Sonata Forms

By the author of

The Classical Style: Haydn, Mozart, Beethoven

Sonata Forms

Revised Edition

by

Charles Rosen

W. W. NORTON & COMPANY NEW YORK LONDON

Acknowledgements

Kuhnau *Sarabande* and *Minuet* are reprinted from the *Denkmäler deutscher Tonkunst* IV, by permission of Breitkopf & Härtel, Wiesbaden.
Excerpts from Haydn's *Piano Trio* H, 15:38 *Quartets*, op. 33, nos. 1 and 6, and the *Kyrie* from his *Harmoniemesse* are reprinted by permission of G. Henle Verlag, Munich.
Excerpts from Haydn's *Symphony* no. 44 and *Symphony* no. 31 are reprinted by the kindly permission of L. Doblinger (B. Herzmansky) KG., Wien.
Excerpt from Haydn, *Symphony* no. 55 are reprinted by permission of Haydn-Mozart Presse/Universal Edition.
The following excerpts by Mozart are reprinted by permission of Bärenreiter-Verlag, Kassel, Basel, Tours, London from the *Neue Mozart Ausgabe: from Zaide:* Serie II, Werkgruppe 5, Bd. 10, edited by Friedrich–Heinrich Neumann, BA 4510, 1957; from *Symphony*, K. 504; Serie IV, Werkgruppe 11, Sinfonien, BD. 8, edited by Friedrich Schnapp and László Somfai, BA 4561, 1971; from *Symphony*, K. 543: Serie IV, Werkgruppe 11, Sinfonien, Bd. 9, edited by H. C. Robbins Landon, BA 4509, 1957; from *Symphony*, K. 297: Serie IV, Werkgruppe 11, Sinfonien, Bd. 5, edited by Hermann Beck, BA 4508, 1975; from *Concerto*, K. 450: Serie V, Werkgruppe 15, Konzerte für ein oder mehrere Klaviere und Orchester mit Kadenzen, Bd. 4, edited by Marius Flothius, BA 4572, 1975; from *Quartet*, K. 465: Serie VIII, Werkgruppe 20, Abteilung 1: Streich-quartette, Bd. 2, edited by Ludwig Finscher, BA 4530, 1962.
Excerpts from Sammartini *Symphonies* no. 6, no. 15, and no. 16 are reprinted by permission of Harvard University Press.
Excerpts from Bruckner's *Symphony* no. 7 are reprinted by kindly permission of Musikwissenschaftlichen Verlag, Vienna.
Excerpts from Bartók's *String quartet* no. 5 are reprinted by permission of Boosey and Hawkes (U.S.A.) and Universal Edition (London) Ltd. (exclusive of the U.S.A.)
Excerpt from Dussek's *Sonata* op. 43 (Prague, 1962) is reprinted by arrangement with Supraphon, Prague.

Library of Congress Cataloging in Publication Data

Rosen, Charles, 1927–
  Sonata forms.

  Includes bibliographical references and index.
  1. Sonata.   I. Title.
  ML1156.R67   781'.52   79–27538

ISBN 0-393-01203-4
ISBN 0-393-30219-9 PBK.

3 4 5 6 7 8 9 0

Contents

To Rachel, Charles Theodore, and Cathy

Preface
to the Revised Edition

FOR THIS REVISED edition, the text has been corrected and enlarged in several places, including an entirely new chapter on codas. I have tried to express my ideas somewhat more boldly and emphasize the points where I depart from accepted wisdom. The role of the subdominant in the second half of a sonata seems to me insufficiently understood; the same is true for the imposing frequency of a move to the relative minor at the end of the development section, although the importance of both was recognized by eighteenth-century theorists.

In my judgment, it is a mistake to view the history of sonata forms as the development of a single form from a single binary pattern. There was no standard form until much later than is generally accepted, and—even more to the point—the evolution of this later standard first-movement form cannot be studied in isolation. It must be seen in the context of other forms like overture, aria, concerto, rondo, and minuet. "Sonata" is a technique of creating a new texture and a new articulation for all these forms.

The reason I have decomposed sonata form into a set of different forms is not to saddle us with a more complex taxonomy, but to make possible a more flexible approach to history. We must beware of taking any of these forms as a kind of real presence behind the individual examples. Stephen Jay Gould's remarks about the chimpanzee are relevant here:

> . . . there are no essences, there is no such thing as "the chimpanzee." You can't bring a few into a laboratory, make some measurements, calculate an average, and find out, thereby, what chimpness is. There are no shortcuts. Individuality does more than matter; it is of the essence. You must learn to recognize individual chimps and follow them for years, recording their peculiarities, their differences, and their interactions . . . When you understand why nature's complexity can only be unraveled this way, why individuality matters so crucially, then you are in a position to understand what the sciences of history are all about.[1]

Sonatas are like chimpanzees.

I am grateful to many people for their suggestions and corrections in this second edition, above all to Joseph Kerman of the University of California at Berkeley, Richard Kramer of the State University of New York at Stony Brook, James Webster of Cornell University, and Robert Winter of the University of California at Los Angeles. Reviews by Professors Kerman and Webster and by Susan Blaustein and David Osmond-Smith have helped me to make necessary changes. What errors and insufficiencies remain are due to my ignorance and obstinacy, and none of the above, of course, should be held responsible. I am deeply indebted to Claire Brook of W. W. Norton for making a considerable revision and enlargement possible.

---

1. Review article, "Animals Are Us," in *New York Review of Books*, 25 June 1987.

Preface

It is good to observe error without disdain: the universality
of men would not have believed it if it had not had so
much relation to, and so many real points of conformity
with, the truth.

SENANCOUR: *Rêveries sur la nature primitive de l'homme*
1802

The book that follows is an attempt to see what can be salvaged of the
traditional view of sonata form. Its insufficiencies, its absurdities,
even, have become steadily more glaring. The more enlightened
musicologists today apply the term to works of the eighteenth century
only prudently, sceptically, half-heartedly, and with many reserva-
tions, spoken and unspoken. Yet I think we still need the term for an
understanding of that period as well as for those which came after. For
this reason I have not considered here the attempts to do away completely with the standard use and substitute new forms of analysis, although it will be obvious that my account of the "three-key" exposition, for example, could not have been written without the inspiration
of Heinrich Schenker. Furthermore, I have not relied entirely on
eighteenth-century theorists (they misunderstood their time just as we
do ours), although I have often found their views stimulating and useful.

The title of this book is plural. That is meant to emphasize that
what was eventually to become the canonic type of sonata form developed along with other forms, which influenced each other and were,

in fact, interdependent. In addition, I have devoted some space to the genres of opera aria and concerto; the development of the variety of related sonata forms extends beyond the domains of symphony, chamber music, and solo sonata. Without aria and concerto the history of sonata forms is quite simply unintelligible.

There is no primary research reflected here. I have relied entirely on printed sources, looked at no manuscripts, ransacked the reserve of no libraries. Such work does not seem to me drudgery—it can be as fascinating as anything else in science or art, but as a pianist I would have the time to engage in it only in the most amateurish way. In the end, an amateur scholar or editor does more harm than a dilettante theorist. A bad theory often provokes an interesting and useful response, but scholarly work once done, however badly, discourages others from going over the same ground again. I am dependent on, and deeply grateful to, those scholars who have made so much of the music of the past available to us.

There is no separate bibliography given here, as it would merely duplicate the relevant material in the magnificent ones available in William S. Newman's indispensable three-volume work: *The Sonata in The Baroque Era, The Sonata in The Classic Era,* and *The Sonata since Beethoven.* I have, however, tried to acknowledge all my specific debts in the footnotes. In the index, the bibliographical references are marked with an asterisk to make them easy to find.

For his helpful suggestions, I am grateful to Dr. Stanley Sadie of the *London Times* and *Grove's Dictionary,* and for his encouragement, to Sir William Glock, who was also kind enough to make more than a hundred changes in the final typescript. Too many of my friends have contributed to my ideas, however, to thank them all as they deserve. Several colleagues and friends made material available, both music and articles, and I should like to acknowledge Dr. Darrell Berg of the St. Louis Conservatory, Professor Lewis Lockwood of Princeton University, Professor Jens Peter Larsen of Copenhagen, Professor John Walter Hill of the University of Illinois at Urbana, Professor Daniel Heartz of the University of California at Berkeley, and Professor James Webster of Cornell University. Professor Henri Zerner of Harvard University made many improvements in the opening chapters. For their reading of the manuscript, I am indebted to Professors Leo Kraft and Sherman Van Solkema of the City University of New York, and to Professor Don M. Randel of Cornell University. My students at Stony Brook gave me a good deal of stimulating help, and I owe thanks above all to Mr. Gregory Vitercik for his ideas and for his aid in gathering material, and to Mr. Robert Curry for his preparation of the particello in the examples from opera arias. The intelligence and kindness of Ms. Claire Brook was a constant help in the final stages, and the reader as well as myself is in her debt.

I ✗ Introduction

ANYONE WHO PICKS up a book on sonata form very likely thinks he already knows what it is; and he is probably right. Since sonata form was defined by theorists in the second quarter of the nineteenth century on the basis of late eighteenth- and early nineteenth-century practice, it has been the most prestigious of musical forms. Here, for the purpose of reference, is the traditional description found in most musical dictionaries, encyclopedias, and textbooks; I give the description in a relatively full and elaborate form so that it will help in recalling the standard terminology.

Sonata form, as that term is most frequently encountered, refers to the form of a single movement rather than to the whole of a three- or four-movement sonata, symphony, or work of chamber music. It is sometimes called *first movement form*, or *sonata allegro* form. In its standard meaning, it is a three-part form, in which the second and third parts are closely linked so as to imply a two-part organization. The three parts are called exposition, development, and recapitulation: the two-part organization appears most clearly when, as often happens, the exposition is played twice (the development-and-recapitulation section is also sometimes, but more rarely, repeated).

The *exposition* presents the principal thematic material, establishes the tonic key and modulates to the dominant or to some other closely related key. (In works in the minor, this will generally be the relative major.) The first theme or *first group* of themes is stated at the tonic. The statement is sometimes immediately repeated (*counter-statement*), and this counter-statement often leads without a break into a modulation or

1

bridge passage: this section ends either on the dominant or, more often with a half-close on V of V. The second theme, or *second group,* is stated in the dominant: it is traditionally supposed to have a more lyrical and tranquil character than the first group, and is sometimes said to be more "feminine." At the end of the second group, there is a *closing theme* (or several closing themes) with a cadential function. The final cadence of the exposition, on the dominant, may be followed by an immediate repetition of the exposition, or by a short transition leading back to the tonic, then followed by the repeat, or—if the exposition is not repeated—by the development.

The *development* section may begin in one of several ways: with the first theme now played at the dominant; with an abrupt modulation to a more remote key; with a reference to the closing theme; or—in rare instances—with a new theme. (In prescriptive accounts of sonata form, generally one new theme is allowed in development sections.) It is in this part of sonata form that the most distant and the most rapid modulations are to be found, and the technique of development is the fragmentation of the themes of the exposition and the reworking of the fragments into new combinations and sequences. The end of the development prepares the return to the tonic with a passage called the *retransition.*

The *recapitulation* starts with the return of the first theme in the tonic. The rest of this section "recapitulates" the exposition as it was first played, except that the second group and closing theme appear in the tonic, with the bridge passage suitably altered so that it no longer leads to the dominant but prepares what follows in the tonic. Longer works are rounded off by a *coda.*

This is what all lovers of "serious" music correctly understand as sonata form. Most of them know, too, that the heyday of the form was the late eighteenth century, and many of them realize that the foregoing description applies rather badly to many eighteenth-century works, and in general misrepresents the practice of that century. They would like to find out from a book on sonata form, I should imagine, what the form actually was in the eighteenth-century, and what its history was—its origin, development, and fate.

These questions seem reasonable enough, on the face of it; but as they are generally put, they are doomed to remain unanswered because they make untenable assumptions. They assume that we can define sonata form so that it will accurately reflect eighteenth-century works, but it is very dubious that a unique sonata form can be so defined even for a single decade of the late eighteenth-century. They assume that a form has a history—in other words, that it is subject to change: but if a form "changes," it is not clear when it would be useful to consider it the same form, although changed, and when we must think of it as a new form altogether. This is not merely a philosophical quibble: there is no biological continuity among sonata forms, and there are many sonatas more closely related to concertos, arias, and even fugues than to other sonatas.

The problem of finding an origin and a history for our form would be well on the way to resolution if we could find a definition for it that would be apt for the eighteenth century. The difficulties one finds with the traditional definition above arise from the conditions in which it was first formulated. It was elaborated principally by Antonin Reicha in the second volume (1826) of his *Traité de haute composition musicale;* [1] by Adolph Bernhard Marx in *Die Lehre von der musikalischen Komposition,* vol. III (1845); and finally and most influentially by Carl Czerny, in the *School of Practical Composition* of 1848. As we can see from the titles of these works, the purpose of the definition was not the understanding of the music of the past but a model for the production of new works. The definition does not work well for the eighteenth century because it was never intended to.

All three of these writers of compositional guides have something important in common: their contact with Beethoven. Reicha, like Beethoven, was born in 1770. He was a close friend of Beethoven when they were young, and they both played in the orchestra at Bonn; some years later, in Vienna, they saw each other again. According to Reicha, they were in contact with one another for a total of fourteen years. Their musical culture and education were very similar. [2] Czerny was Beethoven's most famous pupil, and the most influential teacher of his time: in his theoretical works he claimed to be passing on what he had learned from the masters. In his analysis of sonata form, he relied heavily on Reicha's description. A. B. Marx devoted his life to the deification of Beethoven, and was, indeed, one of the most important agents in the creation of that indispensable myth, the supremacy of Beethoven. This is why sonata form as it is generally known is more or less those compositional procedures of Beethoven which were most useful to the nineteenth century, which could be imitated most comfortably and with the smallest risk of disaster.

The term "sonata form" itself is the invention of Marx. His codification of the form helped to establish its nineteenth- and twentieth-century prestige as the supreme form of instrumental music,

1. Reicha had already given an earlier sketch of the form in his *Traité de mélodie* of 1814. For all these questions of priority in describing the form, see W. S. Newman, *The Sonata since Beethoven,* New York, 1972, pp. 29–36.

2. Berlioz, who studied with Reicha, wrote in his memoirs that he did not think that Reicha and Beethoven had much sympathy for each other; nevertheless, what Reicha described as "la grande coupe binaire" is much closer to Beethoven's procedures than to those of any other composer.

its supremacy guaranteed by Beethoven. Largely a generalization of the procedures of Beethoven before 1812, the description was normative and intended above all as an aid to composition. As the basis for generalization, those aspects of Beethoven (and of Mozart—not of Haydn) which had the greatest interest for the nineteenth-century composer were isolated; these were, principally, the order and the character of the themes. Harmonic and textural matters were consequently pushed into the background, as subsidiary to the thematic structure. The description is essential for an understanding of nineteenth-century music; it gave a model for producing works that is still in force today, although its influence on composers has been on the wane for some time.

The method of defining a form by taking the works of a famous composer as models is rightfully discredited today. Even for the teaching of composition it is a dubious procedure, and it is no help at all in understanding history. What has taken its place is the attempt to define the general practice, what most composers did most of the time within a given generation or decade and within a limited space, a country, region, or even city. Sonata form in the Italy or Mannheim of the 1760s would therefore be what was most commonly done there in that period. The change in the general practice over the years gives us the history of the form.

I may as well lay my cards on the table at once and say that I find the new method as unsatisfactory as the old. The general practice of a period is naturally interesting, but unmediated and uninterpreted it can define nothing. The belief that by itself it has some historical significance is based on a false analogy of music with language (although the relations of music and language are indeed in many other respects intimate and powerful) as well as on a false psychology of the composition and reception of music.

The justification of this method of study is rarely made explicit, merely assumed as self-evident, but it was once put to me forcefully by a music critic on the very subject of sonata form itself. "Take the practice of Haydn in the 1780s," he said. "In the exposition of a symphony, when the dominant is finally established, most composers of the time introduced a new theme. Haydn, on the other hand, reintroduced the opening theme in the new key. Surely in the context of the style of that period, this is a remarkable effect; those who listened to the first performances must have expected a new theme at the dominant and consequently must have received a considerable surprise when the first one reappeared. Without knowing the general practice of the time, and replacing Haydn's works within that context, we shall never be able to understand the effect they made and were, in fact, intended to make."

Let us, in fact, replace Haydn's symphonies within the context of their original performance, and try to put ourselves into the skin of one of the original listeners. In the late 1780s, Haydn wrote nine symphonies for Paris, all commissioned by the Comte d'Ogny: symphonies 82 to 87 (called the *Paris* symphonies) and 90 to 92. The six *Paris* symphonies were all played by the two principal musical societies of Paris, the Concert de la Loge Olympique and the Concert Spirituel: the *Mercure de France*[3] reported in April 1788, that in 1787 "a symphony by Haydn was performed at every concert." They were all printed in Paris in 1788. The later symphonies, 90 to 92, must have been played the next year, as Haydn's popularity was immense at that time, and they were all three printed in Paris in 1790.

What would a music lover at that time in Paris have heard in Haydn's expositions? In the first movements (generally the most elaborate), they would have heard Haydn return to the opening theme in the new key of the dominant in symphonies 82, 84, 85, 86, 90, 91, and 92; in 82, he uses the first theme to continue the establishment of the new key, in 90 he uses it at the end of the exposition as a cadential theme, and in all the others it returns at the point when the dominant is fully confirmed, at the center of the exposition. In the finales, this practice is even more consistent: the first theme reappears at the dominant in all nine symphonies—except for 85, 86, and 92, and in the finales of these three symphonies, a clearly derived variant of the first theme appears in its place.

By the late 1780s most composers used a new theme at the arrival at the dominant (and many already used another theme to initiate the modulation to the dominant as well): Haydn's procedure was markedly eccentric to general practice, and it was remarked as such. In the article already quoted, the *Mercure de France*[4] praised "this vast genius, who in each one of his pieces knows how to draw developments so rich and varied from a unique theme (*sujet*)—very different from those sterile composers who pass continually from one idea to another for lack of knowing how to present one idea in varied forms. . . ." This is the origin of the myth of Haydn's so-called monothematicism—a myth because every one of these movements contain several themes, even if a new theme is not always used to confirm the new key in the exposition. The relative consistency of Haydn's procedure, however, is significant.

A music lover in Paris heard one of these works at every important concert of the season: they were inescapable, and anyone interested in music would proably have heard most of them. The first time he heard the opening theme return at the dominant—just where the average symphony produced a new theme—he may indeed have been sur-

3. See H. C. Robbins Landon, *Haydn at Esterháza 1766–1790 (Haydn Chronicle and Works,* II), Bloomington, Ind., 1978.
4. Quoted Haydn, *Symphonies,* vol. IX, ed. Robbins Landon, preface, page xvi.

prised. If he was slow-witted, he may have been surprised a second or even a third time. After hearing half a dozen symphonies in which this happened in at least one movement (and generally in both the first and last ones), he would have had to be an idiot if he continued to be surprised. In short, the average music lover in the 1780s—as today—listened to Haydn not against a background of general practice but in the context of Haydn's own style. He did not expect Haydn to sound like anybody else; by the 1780s his music was accepted on its own terms. We might, in fact, claim that the more Haydn was heard against general practice, the less he was understood: it is interesting to account for the misunderstandings of the past, but a musicology which seeks to revive and perpetuate them ought not to go unchallenged.

The stylistic unity of the late eighteenth century is often overstated: no doubt, there was then no contrast in style quite as great as that today between, say, Gian-Carlo Menotti and John Cage. Nevertheless, there were many composers in the 1780s whose style was further from Haydn's than that of Benjamin Britten from Igor Stravinsky's, and no experienced amateur of music ever went to hear a new piece by Britten expecting it to sound like Stravinsky. Statistically defined, "general practice" is pure fiction.

Notice that the critic of the *Mercure de France* did not present Haydn as eccentric but as superior: it is not that Haydn and the inferior (according to the critic) composers are working in different traditions or styles, or even producing different forms, but only that Haydn's way of realizing the *expected* symphonic form is more successful. That is because the critic's norms were determined less by what was generally done than by what individual composers were trying or hoping to do, by the stylistic ideals of the period which determined the various possibilities of sonata form. Thematic unity—an expression of affective unity—was still an influential ideal in the 1780s.

If we wish today to describe that late eighteenth-century form which could be realized in such different ways by Haydn and by his contemporaries, then it will clearly not do to use the number and position of the themes as defining characteristics; nor, on the other hand, will it be reasonable to dismiss the thematic structure as merely a surface manifestation of a deeper harmonic structure (although this too has been proposed in our time); the themes and their order clearly had an important role to play.

We may, however, ask what was the function of the second theme appearing at the dominant, and see whether this same function could be achieved by Haydn with a single theme. The device of a "second theme" at the dominant was used often enough by Haydn himself, and the movements in which he used this procedure do not differ significantly in form or nature from the "monothematic" examples. They were in many respects equivalent, and the possibility of that equivalence is one of the determinants of the sonata form of the 1780s. The function, the significance of the "second theme" is, therefore, of greater importance than the frequency of its occurrence. An investigation of the *function* of the elements will enable us to examine the work of all the composers of a period without regard to their deviations from a supposed norm, and will also avoid two traps: first, the definition of form on the basis of a predetermined set of masterpieces, an absurd way of trying to understand music of a large number of composers even if it produced a useful neoclassical model for the nineteenth century; and, second, the postulation of a meaningless statistical abstraction which does not help us to see how the music worked in its own time and still works today (when it does).

II Social Function

THE AGE IN WHICH the sonata forms were created saw rapid and revolutionary changes in the place of music in society. The development of the sonata forms was accompanied by the growing establishment of the public concert. The institution of selling tickets for instrumental concerts grew slowly during the eighteenth century; England seems to have been ahead of the continent. But there is no question of the steady growth throughout the century of an urban and relatively wealthy middle class eager to buy its way into culture. We must reckon, too, with an increasingly conscious need for access to high art, until then mainly the province of an aristocracy and of a professional group.

Before the middle of the eighteenth century, public music was, with few exceptions, vocal music tied to the expression of words (at least in theory and most often in fact as well) both religious and operatic. For centuries, of course, there had been pure instrumental music played in public but it consisted either of arrangements of vocal music, introductions to vocal music (preludes or overtures to church services or operas), interludes between the acts of operas and oratorios, or dance music, which had no prestige whatever (naturally, this did not prevent the creation of masterpieces in that genre). Only religious settings and opera had the prestige of truly public music. Pure instrumental style had grown enormously by the early eighteenth century, but in general, either the works had a court or church ceremonial function, or they were private and professional, for teaching purposes (like the most famous works of Bach and Scarlatti, *Clavierübungen*, *Essercizi*, *Inventions*, *Art of the Fugue*—etudes of composition as well as performance).

8

Nevertheless, there is no question that performances by private societies and in salons were taking on a more public and exploitable character.

The instrumental forms to be exploited were above all symphony and concerto, (and, later, the string quartet, when it became "public" in the 1780s); it is significant that the character of the concerto was almost totally transformed before 1780 by sonata style. This is only partly because the concerto is a specific and limited form and the sonata a general stylistic one; it was above all because the concerto, from the point of view of the neoclassical aesthetics of the late eighteenth century, contained an extramusical purpose—the display of technical virtuosity —which made it in essence inferior to the purer forms of quartet, symphony, and sonata. The concerto retains its relation to the aria: at a public performance of these forms, the soloist and the singer count for more than the composer, the execution for more than the work. This direction of interest is clear in the basic form of early eighteenth-century opera and oratorio, the *da capo* aria. If, in the seventeenth century, music was the servant of poetry, in the early eighteenth both take a humbler place after the singer's art; the *da capo* form accordingly leaves considerable room for the display of virtuosity, including that of improvised ornament.

For the public concert of pure instrumental music, above all symphonic music, proper and apt vehicles were needed, and they were provided by the sonata forms. Orchestral virtuosity was not ignored; it was even richly provided for with opportunities for the controlled crescendo and the *coup d'archet*, but most significantly in the early days of the style, from 1750 to 1780. Orchestral music became, paradoxically, much more difficult in some ways after that date, while the virtuoso element receded into the background. The elaborate passages of spectacular virtuosity for the individual players found in the early symphonies of Haydn disappear in the late symphonies, which are, however, much more complex to play. Virtuosity took second place to music. When the London audience flocked to hear Haydn in the early 1790s and made him a rich man at last, it may have been partly Haydn himself that they were paying to see; nevertheless, it was not Haydn the performer or even Haydn the conductor, but Haydn the composer. Now pure instrumental music alone could be the principal attraction without the seductions of spectacle, the sentiments of poetry, and the emotions of drama, or even the dazzling technical virtuosity of singer and performer. The symphony could take over from drama not only the expression of sentiment but the narrative effect of dramatic action, of intrigue and resolution.

The sonata forms made this possible by providing an equivalent for dramatic action, and by conferring on the contour of this action a clear definition. The sonata has an identifiable climax, a point of maximum tension to which the first part of the work leads and which is symmetrically resolved. It is a closed form, without the static frame of ternary form; it has a dynamic closure analogous to the denouement of eighteenth-century drama, in which everything is resolved, all loose ends are tied up, and the work rounded off.

The sonata was new, above all, in its conception of a musical work as an independent musical object. It was completely written out (unlike the *da capo* aria which left the decoration to the singer), its shape was always definable by a simple contour (unlike the additive and easily extensible forms of the concerto grosso and the variation), and it was totally independent of words (unlike the madrigal and the opera). It is this status of the sonata as an independent musical object, this reification that made possible the commercial exploitation of pure instrumental music. Sonata style, for a brief period, delivered to composers a chance of selling, not a performance or a copy, but the work of pure music itself directly to the public. Shifting the weight of expression from the detail to the large-scale structure, from the performance to the composer's total conception gave the work of music a solid objective status never before conceivable. After 1820, however (and there were already signs before), the virtuoso executants and the virtuoso conductors came into their own.

The sonata forms had a private side as well, above all in chamber music and the solo sonata. We are now tempted to stress the difference between the musical forms of the private sphere and those of the public in the late eighteenth century; nevertheless, the similarities between them are even more remarkable, not to speak of the influence and exchange between one sphere and another. The social development in the private sphere does not, interestingly, provide a contrast with that in the public: the private forms largely serve the same social class as the symphony, but the audience has now become the performers.

The solo sonata belonged to the amateur, particularly the female amateur:[1] that is why the large majority of them are so easy to play. Comparing the sonatas of the 1760s with the keyboard works of the 1730s and 1740s (like Scarlatti's *Essercizi* and the *Goldberg Variations* of Bach), we might infer an extraordinary and universal technical deterioration. For the new nonprofessional performer at the keyboard, however, it was not only desirable to have relatively easy music to play, pieces which did not demand the addition of elaborate ornamentation,

---

1. The keyboard was the most natural and acceptable outlet for women's musical talents and ambitions in the late eighteenth century; some were brilliant professionals for whom Mozart wrote some of his finest concertos and Haydn his most difficult piano trios.

a highly professional skill; but it was also crucial that this music be written in forms that would carry a guarantee of their cultural importance, something the old dance forms could never achieve. The new sonata forms were ideal in their clarity and simplicity and—equally significant—their seriousness.

The demands of an urban class eager to appropriate high culture, coinciding with the development of an efficient tonal system containing the symmetrical range of modulation of the well-tempered scale, and a neoclassical aesthetic, which stressed simplicity and clarity of structure (and considered ornament as fundamentally unnatural and frivolous)— all these contributed to the creation of the sonata forms. For almost two centuries, these forms were to be the basis of the unparalleled prestige of pure instrumental music.

The expressive force of sonata forms was concentrated as much in their structure, the large-scale modulations, and the transformations of the themes as in the character of the themes themselves. This kind of dynamic structure implied, as a corollary, that the traditional improvised decoration added by performers became largely obsolete. Of course, the practice of ornamentation continued—performers have been, in all ages, slow to understand the meaning of revolutionary changes of style. In the most highly organized and complex patterns, the forms created by sonata style conveyed their meaning through the structure, and neither needed, nor indeed could tolerate, decoration. Sonata style represented the triumph of pure instrumental music over vocal music, and as a result, the ruin of the fundamental Baroque theory of musical aesthetics, the *Affektenlehre*,[2] or doctrine of sentiments. A work of music was emancipated, in theory as well as fact, from the expression of one unified sentiment, generally one which could be put into words. In the early eighteenth century, music was considered to reach perfection only when allied to words, but by the 1780s, an amateur of opera, like the novelist Wilhelm Heinse, could write that in opera the music was not the accompaniment of words, but the other way around, a doctrine unthinkable before. The sonata forms had also taken over in opera; only in church music did they meet any strong and durable resistance, and even there, in the end, sonata technique largely triumphed.

There was consequently a basic shift in musical aesthetics, away from the hallowed notion of music as the imitation of sentiment towards the conception of music as an independent system that conveyed its own significance in terms that were not properly translatable. Adam

2. This is not an eighteenth-century word, but a modern one, and a convenient term for identifying a relatively coherent and consistent body of early eighteenth-century musical aesthetic doctrine.

Smith wrote that listening to a work of pure instrumental music was like contemplating a great scientific system, and in 1798 Friedrich Schlegel remarked that pure instrumental music created its own text and that the expression of sentiment was only the superficial aspect of music. This now-apparent ability of music to contain its own significance made it for the Romantic generations of 1790 to 1850 the supreme art, creating an independent world of its own.

Sonata forms made this supremacy of instrumental music in early Romantic aesthetics possible. Their dramatic structure and representation of action contrasted strongly with the unified sentiment expressed in the forms of the earlier eighteenth century: aria, concerto, fugue, and dance, for example. Nor was the structure of a sonata the working out of the latent possibilities of a theme, like that of the fugue; it is the structure, as we shall observe, that confers meaning on the themes. A pure aesthetics of expression was consequently no longer possible in music: the music of the late eighteenth century did not lose its capacity for the expression of sentiment, but an aesthetic which placed the *raison d'être* of music in such expression was unable to cope with a symphony by Haydn. The cracks in the consistency of the doctrine became too obtrusive.

It would be naive to assume that the new social demands made on the art of music created the new forms, or conversely, that the new sonata style made the public concert of instrumental music possible. The institution of the public concert had its own commercial reason for being, the new forms developed according to a stylistic logic of their own, and had their own inherent seductions. It would be best to consider the public concert and the new sonata forms as parallel and concomitant forms of cultural expression; they happily fitted together with extraordinary aptness.

The advantage of the sonata forms over earlier musical forms might be termed a dramatized clarity: sonata forms open with a clearly defined opposition (the *definition* is the essence of the form) which is intensified and then symetrically resolved. Because of the clarity of definition and the symmetry, the individual form was easily grasped in public performance; because of the techniques of intensification and dramatization, it was able to hold the interest of a large audience. Since the expression lay to a great extent in the structure itself, it did not need to be enhanced by ornamentation or by a contrast of solo and tutti: it could be dramatic without the accompaniment of words and without instrumental or vocal virtuosity.

The sonata forms are the product of a long and radical stylistic development: they are, indeed, the essential vehicles of that development. This stylistic revolution plays an important role in the partial emancipation of the composer from the patronage of court and church, by the growing exploitation of the two substitutes for the lost income: the sale of printed music and the public concert of instrumental music. The sonata forms gave a new dramatic power to abstract instrumental music. The gradual supremacy of instrumental music resulted from a movement of emancipation, a liberation of music from its dependence on literature and the visual arts (poetry and stage décor, in particular): pure instrumental music enjoyed a prestige it had never before possessed.

This stylistic revolution came in two large waves: the first, from approximately 1730 to 1765, in which the textures of the previous style were radically simplified; and then, from 1765 to 1795, a second and equally profound change in which the new forms and textures were given a greater monumentality and complexity. The original simplifying movement had to serve various, partly contradictory, purposes: 1) the production of a moderately easy literature for the cultivated amateur musician; 2) the creation of easily comprehended, dramatically conceived forms for public performance; 3) an ever-growing neoclassical taste in all the arts for simplicity and naturalness, opposed to ornamentation and complexity; 4) a new interest in personal, direct expression of sentiment (sometimes called *Empfindsamkeit*) opposed to the objective, complex, emblematic expression of sentiment of the Baroque (*Affektenlehre*). The new sonata forms were supple enough to be adapted to all these ends, and were then considerably transformed in the 1770s and 1780s as their possibilities were exploited, magnified, and finally combined with the contrapuntal techniques of the superseded Baroque tradition. (The specific model of sonata form which crystallized at the end of the century represents the narrowing of a very much wider range of possibilities, and marks the opening of a "classicizing" tendency in musical style.)

The evolution of the sonata forms in the eighteenth century was therefore not an isolated phenomenon. Every one of the formal characteristics that were later to define the sonata is, almost without exception, to be found in all forms, textures, and genres of music from 1750 on—aria, rondo, concerto, minuet, mass—even the fugue and variation did not remain untouched. The changes and transformations of all of these in the eighteenth century cannot be explained by their being married to an independent form called "sonata allegro," but by a general stylistic movement that affected the entire range of music. Nor is it possible to set apart the evolution of the first movement of sonatas, symphonies, and quartets from the equally characteristic and analogous history of slow movements and finales, or to isolate the shape of the large forms from the smaller details of harmony, phrase structure, and rhythmic texture.

That is why there is an irremediable ambiguity about the term sonata, as its meaning vacillates among genre, form, texture, and style. Like fugue, sonata defines a certain kind of texture—or, better, a method of ordering many widely contrasting textures; it indicates a certain kind of instrumental music, but the style and forms of these works extend into the domains of symphony, opera, and church music as well. Perhaps it is neither useful nor feasible to purge the term of these confusions, but they must be exploited prudently.

The ambiguity had already appeared in the eighteenth century in the famous description of the classical sonata by J. A. P. Schulz around 1775, quoted and used by later critics such as Koch and Türk:

> Clearly in no form of instrumental music is there a better opportunity than in the sonata to depict feelings without words. The symphony and the overture have a more fixed character. The form of a concerto seems designed more to give a skilled player a chance to be heard against the background of many instruments than to implement the depiction of violent emotions. Aside from these forms and the dances, which also have their special characters, *there remains only the form of the sonata, which assumes all characters and every expression.* (Italics mine.)[3]

The confusion among style, character, function, form, and genre is implicit. The sonata, which, for Schulz, could be "a due," "a tre," etc., (that is, duo, trio, or quartet as well as solo sonata) here means above all chamber music and *Hausmusik* as opposed to the public genres of symphony and concerto. The contrast with dance music betrays the confusion, for dance music was both private and public, and shows that Schulz is mixing form and genre, social function and expressive tendency. It is no accident that what was to crystallize later as sonata form would be given a name that identified it not with the symphony but with the sonata. The symphony had specific social functions at court which prevented it, before the late 1760s, from reaching complete freedom of expression. For Schulz, the sonata is pure instrumental expression, music liberated from all constraint, social and professional. The various forms it takes are basically neutral, and "can assume all characters and every expression." An historical account demands an understanding of the style that produced these forms and a consideration of its influence on preexisting forms as well.

In the eighteenth century, consequently, there was no notion of an isolated sonata form as such: all that existed was a gradually evolving conception of the composition of instrumental music—a pure instrumental style untroubled by the exigencies of concerto, dance music,

---

3. Translation from William S. Newman, *The Sonata in The Classic Era*, New York, 1972, p. 23.

or opera overture, unhampered by the old-fashioned procedures of fugue and variation. It is significant that eighteenth-century accounts of sonata form are all descriptions of instrumental composition *in general*. As late as 1796, one of the most detailed[4] is entitled "Of melody in particular, and of its parts, members and rules." Perhaps the first description of sonata form to relate it specifically to the sonata appeared in Carlo Gervasoni's *La Scuola della Musica* (1800).[5] In the 1860s sonata form (the name had not yet taken hold) could be called "the form of the free musical development of ideas."[6]

4. Francesco Galeazzi, *Elementi teorico-practici della musica* (1796), one chapter translated and printed by B. Churgin in *JAMS* 21 (1968), pp. 181–99.
5. Piacenza (1800), chapter *Della Sonata*, pp. 464–75.
6. Cf. J. P. Larsen, "Sonatenform-Probleme," *Festschrift Friedrich Blume*, Kassel, 1963, p. 222.

III ✌   Ternary and Binary Forms

FOR MOST OF THE EIGHTEENTH CENTURY, sonata form does not exist as a separate, clearly definable form—and this is true even for most of the second half of the eighteenth century. What does exist is a series of procedures for enlarging, articulating, and dramatizing short patterns of two, three, and four phrases—brief dance forms and song forms. It is with these procedures that most contemporary theorists are concerned. Even so mediocre a theorist as Joseph Riepel recognized in 1755 that large forms function essentially in the same way as small ones. What was to become a standard sonata form very late in the century was essentially a magnification of a restricted number of basic melodic and harmonic patterns. There was nothing very mysterious about the process of magnification. A simple half-cadence or cadence on the dominant became a modulation to V; this modulation could itself be articulated by a half-cadence on V, or more emphatically by a half-cadence on V of V. These cadences were generally set off by a break in the texture—a pause, an accent, a change in dynamics. They could be articulated by borrowing from concerto style a burst of virtuosity just before the cadence. Contemporary theorists were largely, and correctly, concerned with where to put cadences and half-cadences and how to prepare them.

The transformation of these small patterns gave rise to a number of different forms. Some of these resemble what was later to be called sonata form. There is nothing privileged about these seemingly progressive examples; they were only one of several possibilities. Occasionally a theorist will describe a procedure that resembles the standard form of the nineteenth century defined in so many twentieth-century textbooks. It is a misunderstanding to read too much significance into these coincidences. The interplay of possibilities is considerably more important,

16

more meaningful. Any genealogy of sonata form that attempts to derive it from one kind of binary form will only hide the true development. Binary dance form, aria form, and ritornello form each contributed in ways too complex to permit any one of these to take much precedence. Sonata form did not originate by a simple transformation of a single earlier pattern.

By 1790, sonata style had transformed almost all the established forms of early eighteenth-century music. These started in the tonic, went to the dominant, and returned to the tonic with some attempt at symmetry or balance. The most basic of the various formal patterns by which this was effected need to be summarized and defined. It is from the interaction in surprising ways of a number of these forms that the later orthodox form evolved.

Early eighteenth-century forms may be classified roughly as binary or ternary, but we need further precision to understand the mid-century stylistic revolution and the interaction of these forms. I introduce here just enough taxonomy to make the later evolution of sonata forms intelligible.

The basic ternary ABA form is in outline the simpler one. The chief defining characteristic is that the first and third sections are structurally identical—only structurally, that is, because in practice the return of the A in an ABA scheme was traditionally often decorated. The first section, like the third, must therefore end on the tonic. The outer sections, taken singly, are almost always of larger dimensions than the middle (or *trio* —an unfortunate term, perhaps, but there is no other). These two outer sections are not merely the frame, but the pillars of the structure, and the inner one plays a subsidiary role: often more expressive than the outer sections, it contrasts with them, sometimes by a change of mode, but almost always by a reduction of power or stability. In the middle section of a da capo aria, for example, the orchestra is often reduced to a basso continuo alone. After 1720, the tonality of the trio section, in its relation to the tonic of the whole, is one of lowered tension: relative minor and tonic minor predominate. The trio of a minuet or bourrée often has a drone bass, making it more static than the active, more forceful framing sections; or it is simpler in form, less complex in texture, and almost always shorter and less emphatic. The three parts function as *exposition, contrast,* and *reexposition.*

Any sonata form differs fundamentally from ternary form in two ways: 1) even when a sonata form has three clear sections, and the third is thematically a complete recapitulation of the first, these two sections are harmonically absolutely different: the first moves from harmonic stability to tension and never ends on the tonic, while the third is a resolution of the harmonic tensions of the first and, except for subsidiary modulations, remains essentially in the tonic throughout; 2) the middle section of a sonata is not simply a contrast to the outer ones, but a prolongation and a heightening of the tension of the opening section as well as a preparation for the resolution of the third. The essentially static design, spatially conceived, of ternary form is replaced by a more dramatic structure, in which exposition, contrast, and reexposition function as *opposition, intensification,* and *resolution.*

The most important ternary forms, da capo aria and minuet and trio, retain their identity throughout the eighteenth century. In many respects, however, they gradually show an evident influence of sonata style. The trio section of many minuets and scherzos later in the century takes on some of the characteristics of a development, particularly in Haydn's quartets and piano trios; in some of these works Haydn even adds a long developmental coda, as if to offset the static nature of the ternary form. The outer parts and the trio are, taken singly, generally binary forms (after 1730 almost always so) and they assume all the characteristics of sonata style in their own right. The rondo (in form ABAC . . . A) is a specialized extension of ternary form, and the sonata rondo finally becomes a clear and often employed pattern, one perhaps more satisfactorily definable than *first movement* form. Characteristics of the sonata rondo ultimately appear in first-movement forms when these are used as final movements.

Binary form may seem, on the face of it, to be closer to the various sonata forms, and in the traditional historical accounts it is often seen as the immediate ancestor. Binary form is indeed the basic pattern of the individual dance movement of the Baroque suite, and early sonatas and particularly quartets in South Germany often contain a sequence of such dances (the minuet never disappears and eventually becomes a stable element of the quartet and the symphony).

There are three basic kinds of binary pattern in the early eighteenth-century sonata style; for a while they appear to develop independently, but end by borrowing from each other.[1] The "standard" sonata form of the nineteenth century arises in part from all three of them. These patterns may be called "three-phrase," "two-phrase," and "aria" (or "slow movement" or "overture") form; the last will be treated independently in the next section.

"Three-phrase" and "two-phrase" binary form may be simply illustrated by two successive dances from *Partie III* of Johann Kuhnau's *Neue Clavierübung* of 1689. The two-phrase form is the sarabande, the three-phrase the minuet.

---

1. There are a greater variety of binary forms in the early part of the century, but I am concerned here only with those whose symmetrical patterns were absorbed into the new style.

Sarabande

Minuet

Early in the eighteenth-century, many minuets have this three-phrase form, and by 1760 almost all of them do. It remains a stable pattern: phrase 1 has only a weak cadence on V (or often a strong cadence on I) at the double bar; phrase 2 establishes the dominant, sometimes with new material; phrase 3 returns to the tonic with a clear parallelism to phrase 1 and it takes on the character of a recapitulation. When the first phrase has a strong cadence on the tonic (and we still often find this as late as the minuets of Beethoven and Schubert), then the third phrase can be an identical repetition of the first, and the form is close to ternary form or ABA: with repeats it becomes AA BA BA. This three-phrase form is, in fact, so stable that its symphonic expansion is an easy matter and will be briefly discussed later. It should be added here, however, that the three-phrase form is not confined to minuets, but may be found in the Courante from the Suite no. 8 in G major of Handel's set of 1733, in Bach's Two-Part Invention in E major, and in his Aria and Sarabande from the D-major Partita of the *Clavierübung,* Book I, among others. In all four of these examples, the opening phrase has a firm cadence on the dominant; the second phrase contains, after opening on V, a clear orientation to the relative minor, a characteristic of early development sections. The third "phrase" of the Aria from the D-major Partita starts with a retransition from the relative minor, and then has a kind of reverse recapitulation—first reworking bars 9 to 16, and only returning to the opening motif at the end (bar 45). We shall meet this reverse recapitulation later in the century, if rarely.

PHRASE I

PHRASE II

When the opening section of the three-phrase form has a strong cadence on V, it is generally classified as *rounded binary form*. But this term hides an essential kinship with minuet form in which there is a weak cadence on V or even a tonic cadence at the end of the first part. I have deliberately emphasized the parallelism of first and third "phrases" and glossed over the apparently crucial point of whether the first "phrase" ends on tonic or dominant. I have done this because the later minuet form in Haydn, which derives directly from this form (*is* this form, in fact), may have a first half with a cadence either on I or V without apparently affecting the proportions or character of the work.

Three-phrase binary or minuet form may be summarized:

$$
\begin{array}{l}
\text{A} \\[4pt]
\text{I} \longrightarrow \text{cadence} \begin{cases} \text{on I} \\ \text{on V} \\ \textit{on } \text{V but } \textit{in} \text{ I} \end{cases} \ \|: \quad
\end{array}
\qquad
\begin{array}{l}
\text{B} \\[4pt]
\text{V} \longrightarrow \text{cadence on} \begin{cases} \text{V} \\ \text{vi} \\ \text{related key} \end{cases}
\end{array}
\qquad
\begin{array}{l}
\text{A} \\[4pt]
\text{I}
\end{array}
$$

Parts one and three are thematically parallel and sometimes identical; part two (B) is almost always contrasting even when its opening is symmetrical with A.

Simple binary form (or two-phrase form) always has an emphatic cadence on V at the end of its first half, and contains a double and opposing symmetry:

AB:‖:AB thematically
AB:‖:BA harmonically

The melodic structure of the first part is reproduced more or less faithfully by the second and the pattern must be, at least in part, clearly recognizable. (This thematic symmetry is, as yet, only suggested in the Kuhnau Sarabande quoted above, but by the 1720s it is obvious in most pieces in binary form: almost any Allemande by Bach, Handel, or others will do for an example.) The harmonic pattern, however, is reversed in its initial and final points, and the areas they control:

Tonic⟶Dominant:‖:Dominant⟶Tonic

This analytical separation of the harmonic and melodic patterns in binary form prefigures sonata style, but in a sonata form the separation is very differently articulated.

If we take a highly developed example of this thematic symmetry in simple binary form, we can see how the parallelisms work, and how radically they differ from the thematic parallelism of the sonata forms. The Allemande from Bach's Partita in Bb major from the *Clavierübung* has the advantage, for this purpose, of a clearly articulated second theme, and the reappearance of this theme in the second part is revealing (see pp. 22–24).

The two parts are almost equal: 18 bars to 20 bars (the slightly longer second half is the rule in an example of binary form of any complexity). Bars 1-4 establish the tonic in the most ordinary way by I IV V I over a tonic pedal; bar 5 initiates the move to V. *There is no cadence on V until bar 17:* a possible one at the opening of bar 9 is glossed over, and the F-major triad is kept in a six-four position from bars 12 to 14. The second theme at bar 12 makes the modulation to the dominant emphatically clear, but there is no sense of rest, no abatement of flow until the end.

The symmetry and asymmetry of the second part with the first are beautifully conceived. The correspondence of bars is as follows:

```
19  20  22    24  25  26  27  28  29  30  31  33–34  35  37  38
 1   2   4     9  10  11  12  13  14  15  16   7–8   16  17  18
```

The fundamental modulation of the first part is in bars 5 to 9: the return to the tonic in part II is delayed until bars 32 to 34, at which point Bach makes thematic reference to the previous modulatory section (bars 7–9), displaced out of its sequence in the thematic structure. The second theme at the dominant (bars 12 to 16) reappears, not resolved at the tonic, but in the supertonic minor. In the system of eighteenth-century tonality, this gives more than a shadow of resolution: IV is the only alternative to I for opening a final resolution, and the supertonic (ii) is the relative minor of IV, and often used as a substitute for it. No sense of full resolution, however, is achieved here—or, indeed, wanted: the sense of continuity precludes that kind of clear articulation. The subtlety and the sensitivity of Bach's harmonic feeling is unequalled in the early eighteenth century, and it guides the reworking of the pattern here.

The delay of a tonic cadence in part II parallels the delay of a cadence on V in part I: the points of rest are reached at the last possible moment. There is no articulated opposition and therefore no emphatic resolution: the second theme is not played *after* a fully confirmed cadence on V, it is still part of the uninterrupted movement towards V. In consequence, it does not demand a resolution on the tonic, as the second group of the sonata forms invariably will. The reworking in part II of the pattern of the first group, however, includes the motivic elaboration, the modulations, and the faster sequential movement that will become essential characteristics of development sections later in the century. The development section of the early nineteenth-century sonata clearly owes much of its technique to two-phrase binary form (and not only to the three-phrase version, as is sometimes claimed), particularly as the two-phrase form reworks the whole thematic pattern of the first section, and it is fairly common for later development sections to reinterpret the entire thematic pattern of the exposition.

In a sonata exposition, modulation must not only be done, it must be seen to be done. The move to the dominant in the first half of a sonata form is not merely confirmed by a full cadence on V at the end, *but is marked by a decisive change of texture at a point between one-fourth to three-fourths of the length of the exposition:* full or half-cadence, together with a significant pause, brusque change of rhythm, strong accent or any combination of these. This clearly and emphatically distinguishes the area governed by the dominant from that controlled by the tonic, and allows us to speak not just of a modulation as in the simple binary form but of a polarization of the tonic and dominant triads, a "tonicization" of the dominant set into relief. This polarization is reinforced in a variety of ways to be discussed later.

Similarly, in the second part of a sonata form, the resolution of this polarization is also clearly articulated: the exact moment of return to the tonic is always a decisive point set into relief. The means of setting into relief, which is one of the criteria that distinguished the new form, always includes a reappearance of some of the material from the first half—not necessarily the opening measures, although by the early 1770s this had become by far the most common practice. The moment of return, of resolution—generally at the center of the second half of the movement, but often much earlier—is not merely an interruption of continuity, but an essential structural point, so essential that any ambiguity about the exact location of this point, as one often finds in Haydn, is a sensational effect—exactly as a *piano subito* can act as a *sforzando*.

The discontinuities that distinguish the sonata forms from binary form are evidently easier to conceive as stylistic procedures than as definitions of form. These discontinuities are, indeed, the principal preoccupation of the late eighteenth-century theorists—Quantz, Vogler, Koch, etc.; what concerns them most is the character and the placing of cadence and half-cadence within any musical form. The nature of these discontinuities, however, alters the outlines of every form to which they are applied—aria, rondo, concerto—as well as transforming the listener's perception of the proportions of the form. Throughout the eighteenth century almost all music contains an initial movement from tonic to dominant, but sonata style by the 1750s turns this modulation into an overt confrontation of tonalities: that is, the area in an exposition governed by the tonic is firmly distinguished from that governed by the dominant (even when, as often in Haydn, the transition from one to the other may be very extensive), *and all the material played in the dominant is consequently conceived as dissonant, i.e., requiring resolution by a later transposition to the tonic.*

The real distinction between the sonata forms and the earlier forms of the Baroque is this new and radically heightened conception of *dissonance*, raised from the level of the interval and the phrase to that of the whole structure. This transforms all the relationships among the elements of form. It is evident that no sonata form can be either binary or ternary in the normal sense of these terms as applied to Baroque forms, and we shall try to avoid the confusion of that old argument.

The large-scale symmetries of the Baroque style, when they are not completely matter-of-fact, as in ABA or da capo aria form, are often hidden. To take a classic case, the last eight bars of each part of the binary theme of Bach's *Goldberg Variations* are structurally almost identical. The harmonies and most of the melodic contour of one transpose directly into the other:

but it is very difficult for the ear to perceive this identity in performance, as it is obscured by the overlay of ornamentation and the striking change of texture. This kind of hidden symmetry is rare in sonata forms. Sonata style largely dispenses with the simple ABA forms in favor of the reinterpreted symmetries, parallelisms with a difference, inherited from the Baroque, but it makes them always evident.

In a sense, sonata style invented no new forms. It merely expanded, articulated, and made public those it found already lying at hand.

IV ♫   Aria

THE THIRD OF THE important binary patterns to contribute to the sonata forms is rare at first in instrumental music, although examples do exist. Here is one by Handel, the Sarabande from the Suite no. 4 in D minor, published in 1733:

It is a two-phrase binary pattern in which neither phrase is repeated. The two phrases are thematically parallel and harmonically different, but with a harmonic pattern that is not that of simple binary form. The first phrase has a half-close on V; the second starts again on I and closes on I.

This pattern has an extraordinary fortune in the eighteenth century. After 1720 it becomes the almost invariable form of the outer parts of the operatic aria da capo, and remains in force for more than half a century, until the mature works of Mozart; still later examples may be easily found. It is the principal form of the operatic overture, and many slow movements are also written in this pattern. "Aria form" would be a misleading name, as would "overture form," because of the possible confusion with the French overture. We shall call it "slow-movement form": it is not an ideal term, but is, in any case, no worse than "Sonata Allegro" for the standard form.[1] ("Cavatina form" would be even better [see page 40] as it fits mid-eighteenth century usage, but unfortunately the meaning of "cavatina" later changed). The fact that it is used instrumentally most often for slow movements and almost never for first movements is stylistically significant.

This is a good place to summarize the three varieties of binary pattern:

Minuet form (three-phrase)	A I (⟶ V)	B V (or related key)	A or A¹ I
Simple binary form (two-phrase)	A ⟶ B I ⟶ V	A ⟶ B V ⟶ I	
Slow-movement form	A¹ I ⟶ V	A² I ⟶ I	

These patterns endure: they represent three different and relatively stable ways of *reinterpreting a single thematic pattern, however large-scale, into a new harmonic structure,* of symmetrically resolving a structure that moves toward dissonance into one that remains in the tonic. The variety of these patterns and their flexibility is not obscured until, in the early nineteenth century, the classical relationship between tonic and dominant begins to weaken into a more fluid and chromatic system.

The creation and history of slow-movement form is contemporaneous with that of first-movement type (sonata form with development section); moreover, it influences first-movement form, which borrows from it. Consequently the history of first-movement form cannot be understood without a brief attempt to account for slow-movement form, which is not a simplification of its more famous sibling. It is created largely by the same stylistic movement that produced the pattern later to become standard.

It is only in the first decades of the eighteenth century that the da capo aria displaces every other form in Italian opera, and that the splendid variety of aria types that prevailed in the seventeenth century largely disappears. With this standardization comes an expansion and

---

1. The term "sonatina form" has been proposed, but is absurd: I do not know any sonatinas in this form although, no doubt, there are a few. "Exposition-recap. form" proposed by Jan La Rue is too ungraceful to be acceptable.

further standardization of the da capo aria itself. In the late seventeenth century, when the arias remained fairly simple and short, the form is close to what I have called three-phrase binary or minuet form: that is, the middle section goes to the dominant, the outer sections remain in the tonic. One often finds:

A		B		A da capo		
Ritornello	Solo	Ritornello	Solo	Ritornello	Solo	Ritornello
I	I	V	V	I	I	I

With the expansion of the form, and longer, more elaborate arias, the outer section A becomes a binary form with two clear phrases, called for by a repetition of the opening quatrain of the text:

	Ritornello	Solo A^1	Ritornello	Solo A^2	Ritornello
A section alone:	I	$I \longrightarrow V$	V	$I \longrightarrow I$	I

Disregarding the ritornelli, this is slow-movement sonata form (see pp. 106ff). In fact, one or other of the ritornelli are often omitted by the composer, and it is clear that the two solo sections by themselves begin to be conceived as an independent form (although the relation of the orchestral sections cannot be disregarded and will be discussed on page 71 with concerto form.) The return to the tonic, if not found immediately at the opening of the second solo section, occurs a few bars later. This binary structure for the outer sections of an ABA aria becomes monotonously standard by the 1720s.

With this expansion of the A section and the consequent emphasis at the end of its first half on the dominant, the B central member eventually relinquishes its focus on the dominant and moves to tonal areas of weaker intensity, generally the relative minor (vi) and sometimes the tonic minor or the subdominant. By the 1720s, the almost unavoidable stereotype has become (omitting the appropriate orchestral framing sections):

$$
\begin{array}{ccccc}
A^1 & A^2 & B & A^1 & A^2 \\
I \longrightarrow V & I \longrightarrow I & vi & I \longrightarrow V & I \longrightarrow I
\end{array}
$$

which is now the basic ternary form described above, wherein the B section or trio provides a delicate contrast to the generally more robust outer pillars. It is from this point on, of course, that the B section tends to have lighter orchestration than the A sections (although exceptions can be found when dramatic exigencies required it).

An early example of this binary form within the da capo aria, before it becomes the dominant pattern and is merely one among many possibilities, may be found in the air "La mia tiranna" from Alessandro Scarlatti's *Eraclea* of 1700. Here is the A^1-A^2 section complete:

Aria – 31

Disregarding the little opening motto, the vocal part consists of two phrases separated by the tiniest of orchestral interjections; the two are almost identical except that one ends on the dominant, the other on the tonic. This is the form in its primitive beginnings, with all the charm that the primitive can have in the hands of so sophisticated a composer.

Development of the form was rapid, but it took on a surprising character. In order to rewrite at the tonic a thematic pattern that goes from I to V, it would seem that the thing to do is simply transpose everything that was in V to I, and make sure the join does not show by arranging for a convincing transition. But around 1720, when the form was appearing more frequently, although not inevitably, this is not what Scarlatti does. He develops a technique of great subtlety and virtuosity in which he takes a thematic line that goes from I to V, and then delicately alters and reharmonizes it largely within the tonic. The thematic structure is not transposed but retains its original contour, now given a new significance.

Here is the aria "Son costante," from Alessandro Scarlatti's *Marco Attilio Regolo* of 1719. I give the two vocal phrases of the A section written out so that the corresponding bars are placed over each other. The bass and continuo play only in bars 25–27 and 56–67 and largely double the violins and oboes an octave lower (the ritornelli are omitted).

It is not the melody that remains invariant but much of its contour and rhythm: the correspondences are evident and clear upon listening.

More subtle still is the A¹–A² section of the aria "Se di altri," from the same composer's *Griselda* (1721):

This is much closer to simple binary form: a first phrase that goes from
F minor to C minor is paralleled by an asymmetrical double that goes
from Ab major back to F minor. The technique here amounts to a reworking of a motif in which the pitch remains the same but the harmonic significance is radically different. This is naturally a small-scale
effect, almost impossible to transfer to a large structure. With the immense expansion of the aria towards the middle of the century, much of
this refinement is lost—never completely, however, as part of its *raison
d'être* was to keep the singer within a grateful and effective register.

Within only a few years, the relation between the two parts of the A
section began to establish itself with greater clarity, to settle into a few
well-defined patterns. In Leonardo Vinci's *Didone abbandonata* of 1726,
for example, the reworking of A^1 (which goes from tonic to dominant)
into A^2 (which remains essentially in the tonic) is still relatively free,

but the opening of A^2 now falls into three simple forms. As the century advanced, these three patterns were to endure and to become stereotyped: they are used in instrumental as well as vocal forms, and must therefore be looked at in detail. They are:

Type 1) A^2 begins immediately in the tonic, repeating the opening bars of A^1; "Non ha ragione," from act I:

Type 2) A^2 transposes the opening bars of A^1 to the dominant, and then repeats them at the tonic. "Son regina e son amante," from act I. (I have aligned A^1 and A^2 by the words to show that the music is often independent of the verse structure.)

Type 3) A^2 transposes the opening of A^1 to the dominant and returns to the tonic after a few beats. The return of the tonic, therefore, does not coincide with the first notes of the thematic pattern but with

the middle of the opening motif. "Sono intrepido nell'alma," from act II:

The return to the tonic occurs only at the word "alma" here. In a variant of this form, A² starts with the opening not in the dominant, but in the supertonic (ii), returning to the tonic similarly in the middle of the opening motif. "Se dalle stelle," from act I:

I have chosen all these examples from a single opera to show that they coexist happily side by side. The three types—i.e. 1) the immediate return to the first theme at the tonic; 2) the return to the first theme at the tonic only after first playing it at the dominant; and 3) the return to the tonic in the middle of the first theme—are standard by the 1730s and remain almost monotonously so until 1775 and beyond. All three techniques of starting a recapitulation in an aria appear in instrumental forms as well.

The variety of openings for the second solo section A^2, however limited this variety may be, can be ascribed to the ambiguity of its relation to the preceding ritornello. This second ritornello almost always restates the main theme at the dominant. If this was considered sufficient, then the singer could begin again immediately at the tonic: this implied a relatively close and integrated relationship between solo and tutti. However, as the solo sections were conceived more and more as independent self-sufficient forms and the ritornelli as frames, a brief allusion to the dominant for the singer was considered necessary—generally four bars were enough—before the return to I. (Finally, much later, a whole development would precede the return.) This isolation of the solo section is less a formal decision by composers than the result of experience, or so I should think. We instinctively hear the solo sections of a concerto or a song as forming a whole independent of the framing sections of the orchestra or accompanying piano. In a song by Schubert, for example, a four-bar phrase followed by a one-bar extension in the piano is heard only with difficulty as a five-bar phrase; in the same way, the singer of an aria seems to pick up where he or she left off before the intervening ritornello. This accounts for a curious hesitation in aria form between two kinds of binary structure: that in which the second part moves from V to I, and that in which the second part begins at once in I. In general, it may be said that the first solution is never fully adopted in any individual instance—perhaps because this form traditionally entailed a repetition of both parts which was impossible for the aria; and the prevailing description of the outer part of a da capo aria as indistinguishable from binary dance form is deeply mistaken. Usually, in the aria, the return to the tonic is either immediate or only briefly delayed, even when the opening theme is not the vehicle of the return.

It is only gradually from 1720 to 1750 that A^2 takes on the full character of a recapitulation, answering to a corresponding evolution of A^1, which by mid-century assumes many of the qualities of a sonata exposition. A few composers, Handel and Vivaldi among them, used the three stereotyped openings of A^2 more sparingly. In Vivaldi's *Griselda*, most arias in act I are closer to the two-phrase instrumental binary form outlined above, in structure if not in thematic type; only "Alle minaccie di fiera Belua" and "Ho il cor gia lacero" have the second part of A return to the opening material with the pattern I have called type 3; in act II, "Dai Tribunal d'Amore" uses type 2. In Handel's arias, A^2 tends to be a very free development of the thematic pattern of A^1 until almost the end of Handel's life (*Xerxes* presents more standardized forms). In both opera and oratorio, Handel continued the tradition of Alessandro Scarlatti in many respects, and his style, like Bach's (and Scarlatti's in his last years), must have appeared very old-fashioned to most of his Italian and German contemporaries. Other composers, from Lotti to Graun, found the three types of opening A^2 more and more convenient: this opening was generally followed by a short harmonic development[2] and another return to the tonic. When A^2 finally becomes a sonata recapitulation, this development is often displaced and becomes a short section preceding the return. Nevertheless much of A^2's function as a reprise is often in evidence from the beginning of the evolution in the 1720s, when the three patterns for initiating A^2 begin to dominate the aria form.

What characterizes all three types is the return to the tonic either at once or almost at once. They differ radically in this from the binary form of the dance suite described above, which puts off the return for much of the second half, even when the thematic pattern of the first half is repeated. How standard the aria pattern became by the 1750s may be seen by a glance at Graun's *Montezuma* of 1755. (Almost all of the arias in this opera are in what was then called cavatina form: there is no cen-

---

2. A short development immediately after the opening of the recapitulation is also a common feature of instrumental sonata forms by the late 1760s.

tral section and the form is simply A^1A^2 or exposition and recapitulation.) Every one of the eight arias of act I falls into one of the three types described above (although most of them are no longer da capo forms, and omit the trio and repeats). Besides pure representatives of each type,[3] we find an intermediate form between types 2 and 3: A^1 begins by repeating its opening two bars at the dominant, and A^2 merely reverses the procedure:

This is a device that may be found in instrumental work as well. The *Presto* last movement of Haydn's very early Piano Trio in Bb major (Hoboken XV: 38), written at most a few years after *Montezuma*, uses the same device at the beginning of its first and second parts:

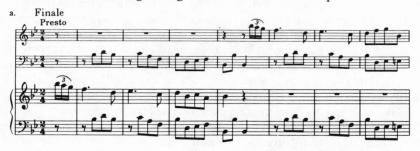

3. Aria no. 7 is type 1, nos. 2 and 4 are type 2, and nos. 3, 5, and 8 are type 3.

b.

and it is also used in the Piano Trio in E♭ major, (first movement, H. XV: 36). This pattern will be treated in more detail in a later chapter (page 155ff).

In most of the operas written from 1730 to 1770 that I know, this standard aria form with its three types of initiating A^2 gives way in one or two places to the demands of the dramatic situation. After the first act, as the drama proceeds, the form is generally handled more freely, and occasionally new ones appear. With the second act of Graun's *Montezuma*, for example, the more rigid forms of the first act begin to yield to more supple and dramatic patterns. The opening chorus and first aria are still of the standard type, but the second aria, "Noi fra perigli," has a central development section; the next aria, "Erra quel nobil core," has new material in much faster tempo between A^1 and A^2 (a striking trio section) and a return of A^2 that begins, like many of the recapitulations of the Mannheim symphonists, only with the fifth bar of the opening material. The final aria of this act, "Da te impara," is most surprising of all: the second part begins with a retransition to the tonic, and a recapitulation in the tonic minor, a trick of the Neapolitan opera composers that we shall meet again in instrumental forms, but rarely. Here is the opening of A^1 (omitting the preceding ritornello), and the ritornello and beginning of A^2:

Aria – 43

a.

Da te im - pa - ra ad es - ser for - le chi più av - vez-zo è a pa - ven-tar

Ge - lo e tre - mo ge - lo e tre - mo e pur la mor-te

b.

RITORNELLO

RETRANSITION

Vuol ven - det - ta la tua of - fe - sa son gia ac - ce - sa -

The return to the tonic and to the opening motif in the aria is generally followed by an immediate move to the subdominant, or to its relative minor ii, and the end of A² is often more elaborate than that of A¹, with considerably more coloratura passagework and a coda. All these characteristics are found contemporaneously in the instrumental forms, too, and are essential to the later sonata forms. It would be useless to try and assign priority for these developments to the vocal or instrumental realm.

Many scholars are reluctant to consider vocal and instrumental forms together. The attempt in the *New Harvard Dictionary of Music* to derive the variant of sonata form which consists only of an exposition and a recapitulation from the Neapolitan overture of the 1730s ignored the widespread use of this form in the arias of the late 1720s. Questions of precedence do not interest me very much, but it is time that we recognize the interplay among different forms and genres. It is generally the same composer who wrote arias and overtures, and the derivation of this from "tri-ritornello form by reduction or elimination of the middle section" proposed in the *New Harvard Dictionary* (following Helmut Hell) is unpersuasive.

In the long run, *opera buffa* was more influential than *opera seria* on the style of the second half of the eighteenth century, above all in the exploitation of contrasting themes and the way the modulation from tonic to dominant was set in relief by breaks in the texture of the buffa aria. These techniques are exceptional in *opera seria* before the 1760s, but the arias of Galuppi's *La diavolessa* of 1755 ("Una donna ch'apprezza il decoro," for example) display them with a mastery which is already a matter of course. Where the writing of operas, serious as well as comic, was crucial for the instrumental composer (and almost every composer wrote operas in the eighteenth century if he expected to achieve any prestige and if he could find a court which would pay for them) was in the experience of dramatically reworking a large-scale thematic pattern: the initial section A^1 that modulated to the dominant had to be reconceived entirely in the tonic, and at the same time the reconception had to remain dramatically effective. A simple transposition was rarely acceptable.

The absorption of operatic style into the pure instrumental genres lies at the heart of the development of music in the eighteenth century: in turn, by the 1760s if not before, the newly dramatized instrumental style was to enrich the operatic stage and make possible a dynamically conceived action, now at last realizable with abstract musical forms. Towards the middle of the century, resolution by transformation, the rewriting of an exposition as a recapitulation, takes place on the largest scale above all in the opera rather than in the symphony. The length of the da capo aria becomes immense, so long, in fact, that more and more frequently the full da capo is not required: instead of a return to the opening with a full repetition of A^1 and A^2, we find a return of A^2 alone:

(Rit.)	A^1	(Rit.)	A^2	(Rit.)	B	(Rit.)	A^2	(Rit.)
I	I→V	V	I	I	Trio		I	I

(Any one of these ritornelli may be omitted by the composer.)

As an example of the sophisticated rewriting of the pattern of an exposition as a recapitulation, I give the beautiful aria from the first act of Jomelli's *Fetonte* (1768) "Le mie smanie," beginning with the last bars of the preceding recitative in order to make the touching harmonic turn of the opening intelligible: the leap from a D-major chord directly to Bb major. I have placed A^1 over A^2 in order to show where the original pattern has been contracted and where expanded.

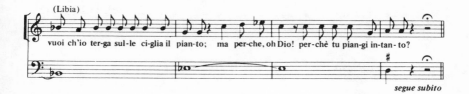

Dal segno

The return starts with the opening of A², and the transformation of A¹ is remarkable above all at bars 69–72 and 90–110. Bar 72 displaces the leap from a D-major chord to B♭ major (V of vi to I) from the opening, and creates the effect of a second return after the first at bar 60. Bars 17–24 of A¹, where the orchestral motif that will dominate the ritornelli is first introduced, have no counterpart in A² (a reasonable omission, as 17–24 function in A¹ above all to confirm and solidify the move to the dominant); but A² introduces a prolongation for four bars (93–96) of the pathetic recitative of bars 41–42 of A¹, and—perhaps the most impressive detail of all—expands the lovely theme that appears at 46–50 into a more deeply expressive phrase (bars 100–106).

The new emphasis on the subdominant (continuous allusion to IV and ii) in bars 76–88 is standard in both instrumental and vocal recapitulations throughout the eighteenth century. Like most trios, the B section (from bar 118) has a harmonic character of lesser tension (almost entirely in the relative minor and the subdominant), while remaining expressive. It introduces new material. The ending of this trio section in the relative minor reintroduces the move from a D-major chord to B♭ major.

The character of the transformations at bars 69–72 and 90–110 is purely operatic in origin, with a clear relation to recitative. Nevertheless, this kind of transformation has its counterpart in pure instrumental style. A dramatic interruption of the thematic pattern was often introduced into the recapitulation, often towards the beginning. Here are the first eight bars of the exposition and corresponding bars of the recapitulation of Haydn's Piano Sonata in C minor (H. 20) of 1771 (three years after Jomelli's *Fetonte*):

a. Moderato

5

b. [RECAPITULATION]

69

The startling interruption at the beginning of bar 76 gives this passage its operatic air. It is a technique that remains important for a long time: among its greatest examples are the recitatives at the opening of the recapitulation of Beethoven's *Tempest* Sonata (op. 31 no. 2, first movement) and the transformed second group in the recapitulation of opus 111. The interruption of continuity at the beginning of the reprise of Haydn's C-minor sonata is derived only indirectly from opera: its direct ancestor is the work of C. P. E. Bach, who made a specialty of such dramatic breaks in texture. The frequent use of recitative phrases in C. P. E. Bach's instrumental works, however, shows that his style did not remain untouched by opera seria. In turn, opera seria felt his influence: the work of Jomelli, after he settled at the court in Stuttgart in the late 1750s, reveals a kind of motivic construction that relates to the large form in a way that would not be easy to parallel in the work of his contemporaries who remained in Italy. In his *Olimpiade* of 1761, for example, the aria "Sò che fanciullo Amore" uses a short but highly characteristic motif in descending thirds (with a canonic imitation) as an opening theme, inverts this at the dominant for a second theme, and then presents a rapid diminution of the motif as a closing theme. This was a typical North German means of elucidating a sonata structure: it spread southward very quickly. The interchange between pure instrumental and operatic forms took place throughout the century, and was one of the principal agents of stylistic development.

As we have seen, the enormous expansion of the da capo led mercifully to a slightly abridged version omitting the repetition of A^1:

$$A^1 \quad A^2 \quad B \quad A^2$$
$$I{\to}V \quad I \qquad\quad I$$

Relatively early we can find examples of a further truncation, the omission of the first performance of A^2, so that B follows hard upon A^1. This results in

A^1 Exposition	B	A^2 Recapitulation
tonic ⟶ dominant	tonic minor relative minor or relative major etc.	tonic

The B section, although placed between an exposition and recapitulation, may be distinguished from a development section in various ways: by its being in a different tempo from A^1 and A^2 (generally slower) and with a different time signature, by its harmonic character and its presentation of new material of a more lyrical temper, and in general by opening not as a continuation of the polarity of the exposition A^1 but as something new and different, after a fermata. There may sometimes be a few bars of development between A^1 and B, but then B enters as an interruption.

The interruption is often of surprising dimensions, but this only attests to the integrity of the relationship between A^1 and A^2. An extraordinary demonstration of this relationship is given by scene 8 of act II of Jomelli's *Fetonte*. The hero's aria (allegretto, 2/4), "Tu parla, tu digli," is interrupted at the end of A^1 when he tries to leave and is intercepted by Libia. A trio of more than sixty bars follows, (andante, 3/4), after which the original tempo returns and the recapitulation A^2 finally takes place. Dramatic tension is symbolized by the formal tensions characteristic of the sonata form: the harmony is unresolved until the recapitulation of the opening half of the aria is achieved. It is large-scale experiments of this kind that made the even greater breadth of Mozart's forms possible.

There are, in sum, three versions of the da capo aria by the 1750s, all of which can coexist happily, side by side, in the same opera. They are, first, the full version:

$$A^1 \ A^2 \ B \ A^1 \ A^2$$

the slightly abridged form, sometimes called the *dal segno aria* (as it goes back to a sign at the beginning of A^2):

$$A^1 \ A^2 \ B \ A^2$$

and the shortest form, the sonata form without development but with a central trio section:

$$A^1 \ B \ A^2$$

This demonstrates that the sonata form with central trio section is not a hybrid—an intrusion of ternary form into a binary sonata—but a natural evolution. In every one of these patterns, the relation of A^1 to A^2 is that of a sonata exposition to a recapulation.

All of these variants gradually give way in the 1770s and 1780s to the aria with development section (a form that has links with the concerto, and will be treated briefly with that genre); in other words, the da capo aria, like almost everything else in the eighteenth century, gradually turns into pure sonata style. Mozart's *Ascanio in Alba* (K. 111) of 1771 still had one full da capo form, no. 21, "Dal tuo gentil sembiante," but the composer himself cut out the B section and the da capo before the first performance. "Spiega il desio, le piume," aria no. 19 of this same work, is a dal segno aria with only A^2 repeated. This form is rare in Mozart, although he wrote another example as late as 1778, with K. 295, "Se al labbro mio non credi" (an aria to be inserted in Hasse's *Artaserse*).

The aria with central trio section occurs more often in Mozart, although still relatively infrequently. There is one in *Ascanio in Alba* (no.

16, "Ah di si nobil alma"), in which the central change of tempo is less surprising since the A¹ A² sections are already both made up of contrasting tempi, adagio and allegro. There is a beautiful example in *Idomeneo* (no. 27, "Nò, la morte") of 1780, and, the year before, two in a row in the magnificent but unfinished *Zaide* (K. 344): no. 13, "Tiger, wetze nur die Klauen," and no. 14, "Ihr Mächtigen seht ungerührt."

I give the first and most impressive of *Zaide's* two arias to show how a sonata form with central trio worked in the 1770s, and to show, as well, the way in which the central part of what was essentially a ternary ABA form began to take on some of the functions of sonata style.

Aria – 63

Aria - 65

After the end of the exposition, bar 58, there are four bars of development using the initial motif of bar 3 combined with that of bars 37–38, but played in 59–62 in a modulating sequence of striking dramatic character. The larghetto that follows in the submediant E♭ (prepared elliptically, as a modulation at bar 62 ends in the dominant of C minor) presents new material, new rhythm, and a new tempo. It has not, however, progressed more than ten bars before it begins to assume the harmonic function of a sonata retransition, to prepare the return to the tonic G minor. With bar 70 the syncopations begin to approach the more agitated texture of the outer sections of the aria: these syncopations, emphasized by the accents, become more pervasive in bar 74; from 95 to 98 they lead directly back into the allegro assai.

The partial transformation of the delicate but expressive contrast of a trio section into a more dynamic relation to the whole form appears earlier in the century; it becomes most obvious in the abridged form of the da capo aria, as here, when the trio follows hard upon A^1 with its opposition of tonic and dominant. When the trio follows A^2 (in the full or partially abridged da capo form), it begins after a resolution in the tonic: its function as the center of a true ternary form is therefore unimpeded. In the abridged form it has an ambiguous place: it follows the polarity of tonic and dominant, a large-scale structural dissonance which requires either immediate resolution, or prolongation and retransition to resolution—in other words, a development section. The trio, in its original form, does neither; when it occurs for dramatic reasons, however, it begins to be absorbed into the sonata aesthetic, and takes over some of the developmental characters. This has its analogue in pure instrumental works, where the transformation of ternary forms is often, indeed, far more thoroughgoing.

The ambiguous significance of the central trio in a sonata form is wonderfully displayed by 1782 in Mozart's *Abduction from the Seraglio*. The overture is in the form we have been examining: A^1, presto, ₵, C major to G major; B, andante, 3/8, C minor; A^2, presto, ₵, a recapitulation which turns the original modulation to G major into one back to the tonic, but in the minor mode with a pause on a dominant pedal. The opera then opens with the central section B of the overture as an aria, *but now reconceived in the major mode.* The aria serves as a resolution of the overture, a resolution of its unfinished ending and its central section at one and the same time. Mozart uses the ambiguous function of the trio to create an extraordinary manner of integrating overture and opening scene.[4]

From this brief and oversimplified sketch of the evolution of slow-movement form (sonata-form-without-development) in the operatic

4. The stylistic sense that made this possible is at work even more remarkably at the opening of *Don Giovanni:* the integration of overture and opera is achieved tonally by the following symmetry:

Overture	Scene 1	Scene 2
D minor—D major→ F major (unresolved)	F→ F minor (unresolved)	D minor

(See Rosen, *The Classical Style,* New York, 1972, pp. 302–03.)

aria and of some of its contacts with other forms, it can be seen that it is not an abbreviated nor a simplified version of sonata form. We may conclude, further, that we cannot label something a development section merely because it is to be found sandwiched between an exposition and a recapitulation. The functions of a development section are the essential consideration: we must first ask of any middle section how it works—indeed, how it acts. The answers are not always likely to be straightforward.

V ⅕   Concerto

CONCERTO AND ARIA are closely related forms: often, in fact, identical. An extreme instance of this identity is the sinfonia concertante for voice and instruments: two examples by Mozart are the brilliant "Martern aller Arten" from the *Abduction from the Seraglio* and the lovely "Et incarnatus est" from the C-minor Mass; in both, the solo instruments of the orchestra collaborate with the soprano even in the cadenza.

Concerto and aria pit individual against mass, solo against tutti; that is the essence of both forms.[1] How the alternation of tutti and solo passages was organized changed radically in the eighteenth century; it became part of sonata style generally. Like the aria, the concerto did not just become sonata passively; it also helped shape the sonata forms and contributed some of their most important elements.

Towards the middle of the century the number of tutti and solo sections in the instrumental concerto and their harmonic character begin to become standardized—one might say rationalized. The mid-century settled on three solos framed by four tutti or ritornelli. The first solo goes from tonic to dominant,[2] the second generally ends in the relative minor, and the third remains in the tonic throughout:

R	S	R	S	R	S	R
I	I→V	V	→vi	I	I	I

---

1. See D. F. Tovey, "The Classical Concerto," in *Essays in Musical Analysis,* vol. 3, London, 1936–44.

2. This is a good example of the standardization of sonata style. Earlier concertos, including several by C. P. E. Bach, may have a first solo that goes to the subdominant, but this possibility seems to have disappeared after about 1770.

(This is a form best exemplified in the concertos of Johann Christian Bach.) What will concern us here are the relations of the first ritornello to the first solo, the character of the second solo and the nature of the framing devices so basic to the form.

The later eighteenth century was of two minds about the first ritornello. Thematically it always presented most, although not all, of the main ideas of the piece—but harmonically? Two possibilities were open: it could contain a modulation to the dominant, or stay in the tonic throughout. In other words, the first ritornello could take on the character of a sonata exposition, or it could keep its older concerto function, in which the first and last ritornelli were the same—the older form being essentially an ABA form in which the B was much longer and more complex than the outer frame.

Both solutions were awkward, which is why the eighteenth-century theorists were never entirely clear about them.[3] Nor were the composers. Retaining the framing character by having the final ritornello completely repeat the first turned out to be more and more impracticable as the form expanded. The opening ritornello became grander and more symphonic, too long and too ambitious to repeat at full length at the end. In general, composers settled for playing only the final paragraphs of the opening tutti at the end of the movement: the cadential portions served as a frame, and the first ritornello consequently retained its final cadence in the tonic. It was evidently essential to the sense of the frame that the first and last sections should end not only with the same thematic pattern but in the same key. The identity of key is, in fact, even more important than an identity of thematic content: the final cadence of the first ritornello is still generally a tonic cadence even when it uses a different thematic pattern from the cadence that will close the movement. There were, however, experiments towards mid-century with an opening ritornello that ended on the dominant (e.g., the last movement of Wagenseil's Concerto in F Major for Cembalo), but they were not influential. It is significant that as the century went on and the tonic-dominant polarity of the sonata exposition became more highly articulated, the concerto largely abandoned even these rare essays that imitated the sonata exposition by closing the orchestral exposition in the dominant. The tonic cadence was not only reaffirmed but made considerably more emphatic. The first ritornello continued, as before, to begin and end in the tonic: this requirement appears to lie at the heart of the eighteenth century conception of the

3. See the fine article "Theme, Harmony, and Texture in Classic-Romantic Descriptions of Concerto First-Movement Form," by Jane R. Stevens in JAMS 27 (1974), pp. 24–60, which describes the way eighteenth-century theory fudged the basic outlines of concerto form, and follows this with a definitive demonstration of the poverty of most of the theory after 1800.

concerto, an aspect of ternary form that it never lost. But as the first ritornello expanded to symphonic length, casting all of its themes and motives in the tonic was not a simple matter. If the beginning and the end needed the tonic, the middle of this opening tutti seemed to admit more freedom. It was, to be sure, difficult to handle a succession of themes all in the same key without the danger of monotony. Almost all music in the eighteenth century goes—sooner rather than later—to the dominant. So the ritornello as sonata exposition began to appear, in which the second group of themes moves to the dominant, and then—and here was the rub—moves back to close in the tonic before the solo exposition.

The clear desire for symmetry, for having both first and last tutti sections end identically on the tonic, created the problem. An opening ritornello entirely in the tonic with no modulation—as in the older concerto form—implies that something will happen, creates an expectation of action. By contrast, a ritornello that starts on I, moves to V and then returns firmly to I with all dissonance and tension resolved is an action completed. It must be remembered that the tonic close of the opening tutti must be elaborate enough to serve as the end of the whole piece. Its appearance at the end of the first section therefore resolves any harmonic polarity and tension that may already have been set up, resolves them too swiftly for the scale of the piece: establishing a tonic-dominant opposition makes any impressive set of tonic cadences following it appear like a complete resolution, and it is too soon in the work for that. When the exposition of a symphony or sonata is repeated, the return to the tonic of the opening bars may be interesting, but it can never be elaborate: it is always immediate, unstressed, and even, ideally, perfunctory.

This is why the opening ritornello as sonata exposition never gains a firm foothold, in spite of its attractions. It always, however, remained a possibility. Mozart used it on a few occasions (principally in the Piano Concerto in Eb major, K. 449), and otherwise retained the older conception[4] of remaining in the tonic throughout the opening tutti. Beethoven also returned to the older form in the fourth and fifth piano concertos, holding back the first fully established modulation in both works until the solo exposition.[5] How Mozart and Beethoven enlivened a long section entirely in the tonic need not concern us here, except to mention

---

4. K. 466 begins the modulation but abandons it after two bars and returns to the tonic area.

5. The first two concertos of Beethoven have opening orchestral expositions that modulate and return to the tonic, with a final page that is also used for the end of the movement later. With the third concerto, Beethoven abandons the symmetrical ending, writing a coda for piano and orchestra in place of the final ritornello: the opening ritornello moves emphatically to III and just as emphatically back to i.

the most imaginative of their solutions: the rapidly modulating theme that establishes none of the keys it touches upon, and which therefore does not attack the authority of the tonic, but merely gives it a vivid chromatic sonority.

The closure of the opening tutti on the tonic, therefore, not only determines the shape of this first section as a whole, it also determines the significant structure of the concerto (and the aria as well, for which the foregoing holds true): it places the dramatic modulation in the province of the soloist, it firmly sets off the ritornello from the initial solo section, and it provides a well-defined frame. Even when the solo entrance in Mozart and Beethoven makes a special effect by interrupting the orchestra, what it interrupts is a tonic cadence.[6] In the beginning of the first solo from Mozart's K. 450, the orchestra finishes its elaborate cadence one bar after the piano enters:

---

6. K. 467 seems to be an exception, but the orchestra is interrupted only after a cadence so final that it is repeated at the end of the movement: in other words, the ritornello is actually concluded several bars before the solo entrance.

Indeed, concerto style is particularly rich in apparently final cadences: Mozart generally uses a string of them in a row at the end of the first tutti. He needs them later: one to follow the last solo, but to precede the cadenza, and at least two more to follow the cadenza and end the movement in grand style.

When the fifteen-year-old Mozart arranged several sonatas of Johann Christian Bach as concertos, he had to start by transforming the sonata exposition into a ritornello. He did three things: he removed the modulation to the dominant, transposing the second group to the tonic; he cut a part of the second group in order to allow the soloist to have some new material of his own, and, finally, he added some more cadential material at the end. These three points remained essential to Mozart's conception of the concerto until the end of his life.

Christian Bach's sonata style was already deeply influenced by concerto textures, but there was still not enough cadence for Mozart. To make the Sonata in Eb major, op. V. no. 4, of Christian Bach into a Concerto (K.107), Mozart added the following elaborate cadence to the first theme:

which he used again later to introduce the cadenza. At the end of the ritornello, after a thorough rewriting of the second group in the tonic, he added:

which he used later to close the movement.

In his arrangement of J. C. Bach's Piano Sonata in D major, op. V no. 2, as a concerto, Mozart articulated the form as he added the orchestral accompaniment. The extra parts are in general added with a light hand. If we note the few places where the scoring is heavy, it will indicate those structural points of a sonata form that Mozart felt necessary to set in relief. After the opening ritornello, they are:

1. The half-cadence on V of V before the introduction of the second group.

2. The cadence on V at the end of the exposition.

3. The cadence on the relative minor (vi) at the end of the development—the most common cadence of an eighteenth-century development section.

4. The half-cadence on V eight bars later at the end of the retransition, before the return of the main theme on I.

5. Only moderately heavy scoring at the end of the recapitulation of the first group, cadence on I.

6. Cadence on 6/4 of I, introducing the cadenza.

7. Final ritornello.

It was so easy for the fifteen-year-old composer to emphasize these articulations because concerto texture had already been long adopted as a means of clarifying the form in chamber music and symphony. A mimesis of the tutti-solo alternation is standard throughout late eighteenth-century music of whatever genre.

The contrasting cadential material of orchestral character was crucial to the evolution of the sonata forms: it allowed them to expand, articulated the important structural points, defined the contours. It derives, not from the symphony or chamber music, but from concerto and aria: it gradually permeated symphonic and chamber styles. Another form of cadential material important to the evolution of sonata forms also derives from concerto and aria; it is not orchestral but individual—instrumental as well as vocal: cadential virtuosity, the scales, flourishes, and trills that mark the end of a solo section. Here are the first eight and last nine bars of the first violin part in the exposition of Haydn's Quartet in G major, op. 17 no. 5, to show the difference in texture:

a. FIRST 8 BARS

b. BARS 25–33

The leaps down to D and then up two octaves in bar 31 are pure mimesis of those beloved by eighteenth-century sopranos anxious to display their wide range, like the singer Mozart indulged so generously when he wrote the part of Fiordiligi. I chose an example by Haydn rather than one by Mozart or Christian Bach; the latter are both so deeply influenced in all their works by concerto technique that it is only too easy to find examples of their articulating the form of a sonata with this kind of virtuoso passagework: the extended cadential gesture was second nature to them.

It was preserved by later composers:

The end of the exposition of Beethoven's opus 53 shows the virtuosity, the closing trill, and the series of cadences derived from concerto style.

The alternation of solo and tutti in concerto and aria makes the articulation of these forms profoundly different from any other contemporary forms. The difference may be seen at its most striking if we remark the distinctive ways of setting off the end of the exposition. In an eighteenth-century quartet, symphony, or sonata, the end of the exposition is almost always marked by a rest—the music stops for a brief and measured moment: in the concerto, the end of the exposition runs directly and continuously into a new texture, the opening of the second ritornello. There is no break between solo cadence and the entrance of the full orchestra.

It is obvious that these are equivalent procedures: the important thing is that the end of the exposition be set off by a break in texture. The equivalence may be easily demonstrated. The end of the exposition is only the last structural point to be articulated in the first half of a sonata form, and the move to the dominant must be set in relief before that. In the first solo of a concerto this moment is often preceded by a brief interruption from the orchestra, *forte,* and the modulation is followed by another interruption. Here is the end of the first group and the transition to the second in Mozart's Concerto in Bb major, K. 238 of 1776; the moment before the modulation is emphasized by the or-

chestra in bars 45–47, and the modulation itself is confirmed orches-
trally in bar 54:

In the concerto, the alternation of solo and tutti is used to articulate the sonata, and this technique is, in turn, borrowed and imitated in symphony and chamber music.

The end of the exposition in aria and concerto, however, has an inescapable ambiguity, which arises from the character of an inner frame: does the entrance of the tutti end the exposition, or begin the development? This is not a quibble about terminology, as there are two ways of starting the second ritornello, one of which faces forward, the other backward: it can start either with the opening theme or with the closing paragraph of the first tutti, now played at the dominant. The former is the older tradition and gives to each of the ritornelli a symmetrical opening. Mozart uses this form in the piano concertos only once, in K. 415; otherwise, he uses the more modern form, and the tutti at this point replays either the closing themes of the first ritornello or the end of the first group (in K. 459, the tutti starts, not with the first theme, but with a variant of it in the solo exposition).

To open the second ritornello with the first theme at the dominant implies a new beginning: when, on the other hand, the orchestra enters with the closing themes (the more modern technique, developed in the 1760s), it rounds off the solo exposition. In that case, however, one expects a firm cadence on the dominant. If the cadence is withheld, the ambiguity reappears; the apparent rounding-off was a new beginning after all, a beginning underlined by the change from solo to orchestral texture. We can see Mozart rounding the solo exposition off in most of the concertos (K. 414, K. 491, etc.), and Beethoven in his first two; but Mozart plays with the ambiguity in K. 488 and K. 595, and turns the rounding off in K. 450 into a new beginning by picking up the last phrase of the second ritornello with the second solo entrance:

Here, applied to the concerto, is a sonata technique derived from the symphony and quartet, perfected above all by Haydn: the development opens by reworking the last phrase of the exposition, and so overrides the break between the two sections.

The particular character of the second ritornello—transition between two solo sections, end and new beginning at one and the same time—accounts for the evolution of the sonata form without development as a basic aria form. We might say, putting it as simply as possible, that a development section postpones resolution for a moment, and that the aria form had no need for this, as the second orchestral tutti already postpones the tonic return. Most development sections of instrumental works in early sonata form tend to begin with the first theme at the dominant; in the aria, this, too, is done by the second ritornello. I have put off considering the role of the orchestral sections of the aria until here, because the concerto form is a necessary help in elucidating this point.

The pattern most often found for the aria from 1730 to 1760 is:

R 1	Solo 1	R 2	Solo 2	R 3	B	
A	A elaborated	A	A elaborated + coda	A		+ da capo
I	I——→V	V	I	I	vi	

(R = ritornello and A = thematic pattern with opening theme and cadential themes)

in which solo 2 may begin with a brief retransition from V to I, but reaching I very quickly and reworking the pattern of solo 1. A development section prolongs the polarity of the exposition by prolonging the tension of the dominant, in ways that extend beyond the banal presentation of the first theme at the dominant. This function is fulfilled admirably by the second ritornello. It cannot, however, encompass the other characteristics typical of the development section—the thematic development proper, the fragmentation of motif, the sequential modulation, and the retransition. The function of retransition was often assumed by the opening bars of the following solo section, but as for the other functions, a composer of opera who needed them for dramatic reasons was forced to work them out in some other way—sometimes in the B section, an unsatisfactory makeshift, or in a real development section. For this reason, an aria with a separate solo section between A^1 and A^2 appears with ever greater frequency in the 1750s and 1760s, particularly when da capo form is abandoned. Nevertheless, the two-part aria, with or without B section and da capo, is still the standard form until the 1770s, when the aria with development section, or "sonata-aria" becomes a formidable rival. "Concerto-aria" would perhaps be an even better name for this form, as the two are essentially identical at this point. The aria is, in fact, heavily influenced by the concerto as far as the second solo is concerned, and we must pause to examine this very briefly, particularly as the development section of the instrumental sonata does not in turn escape the influence of concerto form.

The second solo of a concerto may start with the main theme played at the dominant—but as often as not it will do something quite different, and begin with new material, a theme of expressive character that has not yet appeared either in the ritornello or the first solo. The presentation of entirely new material is equally marked in the concerto-aria, particularly as it evolves after 1770: there are many such "development" sections that have, in fact, no thematic development of material from the exposition at all. Yet this form cannot be confused with an aria with central trio, like the one quoted from *Zaide* (p. 59ff). The central sections of such arias as "Se il tuo duol" or "Fuor del mar" (nos. 10 and 12 from *Idomeneo*) function as development sections in every respect except the thematic: in harmonic structure, harmonic rhythm, and texture, they are true developments. They prolong, indeed increase the tension of the exposition, and prepare the return. I give the second ritornello, second solo, and third ritornello of "Fuor del mar"; this is as good a place as any to display the nonthematic aspects of a development:

me _ no. se al nau _ fra _ gio è si vi _ cino il mio

cor, qual rio de _ sti _ no or___ gli vie _ tail nau _ fra _ gar,

or___ gli vie _ tail nau _ fra _ gar, il nau _ fra _ gar, il nau _ fra_

gar.

cresc.

p

Fuor del mar ho un mar in se _ no,

f p

The solo section contains material congruent with that of the exposition, but at no point identifiable with any earlier motif (to spare the space I do not print the exposition, and the reader will either have to take my word for this or else look up the whole aria himself, which should only give him great pleasure). The texture—fragmentation, sequential harmony, wide-ranging modulation—is that of the sonata development. It is, indeed, not only in the operatic aria that Mozart writes a development section with entirely new material, but also in piano sonatas like K. 283 in G major and K. 330 in C major: the developments contain material that makes no direct allusion to the exposition, although blending very well with what went before. The F-major Sonata, K. 332, has a true thematic development section, but one which opens with a new theme:

This goes well with the opening theme:

but that is a matter of decorum: one is not transformed into the other, although they have certain similarities in contour and harmonic rhythm. This practice is a clear derivative from concerto form.

The second solo of a concerto generally contains a good deal of rhapsodic arpeggiation (of the kind still used by Beethoven at the opening of the development of the Piano Concerto in C major and made more dynamic in the *Emperor*). Here is a staggeringly uninspired example of the technique from the second solo of the Concerto in F major by Wagenseil, already mentioned on p. 72:

and so on for about a dozen bars more. The voice-leading of bars 45–47 is so atrocious that one would like to imagine a printer's error, but not even emendation would help much. The performer, one presumes, was not supposed to repeat the opening figuration literally, but to vary it: the harmonies, which are interesting enough in themselves, are merely a skeleton on which the harpsichordist or pianist was to improvise an interesting and impressive texture. The continuously changing harmony and the air of improvisation of such passages became important to sonata style in solo piano music and even in quartets.

I give in full the second solo of the Concerto in Bb major of J. C. Bach (op. XIII no. 4) published in 1777, as an example of this essential part of a concerto structure, so that the differences and similarities of a second solo and a sonata development can be more easily appreciated, and I add a few quotations from the exposition and recapitulation to make the central solo intelligible.

The first movement has a main theme with a unison opening and a graceful answer:

A later theme of the first ritornello (which stays throughout in the tonic) never appears in the first solo:

(A theme which appears in the orchestral exposition but not in the solo exposition, and is taken up by the piano later in the work was a device that Mozart adopted several times—e.g. the Concerto in C major, K. 503.) The piano, however, has a second theme of its own:

followed by a considerable amount of brilliant passagework. Still another theme appears after a decisive cadence:

and further brilliance follows. After a final flourish the orchestra reenters, and the second ritornello transposes to the dominant the opening four bars and the closing theme of the first ritornello, making a huge cut between them.

The second solo starts with a fine new theme:

and repeats it at once in the tonic:

We recognize this procedure from the aria, and will find it again in quartet, symphony, and sonata. The second solo of the aria (in what I have called type 2) plays the main theme at the dominant, repeating it at once at the tonic: the pattern is so habit-forming that J. C. Bach does it here with his new theme. (This return to the tonic with the second phrase of the development will be discussed briefly later.) The anomaly must be noted, however: the aria has two solo sections, the concerto three, and the return to the tonic so soon after the opening of a section would appear to be better adapted to a final section than to a central one, or "development." But there is as yet no development in this concerto of J. C. Bach.

The return to the tonic is followed by the standard section of arpeggiation, less deadly than in Wagenseil (although the move to the tonic 6/4 chord in bar 123 is clumsy enough):

The development is not thematic in nature, but harmonic and textural in its sequential modulations and fast-moving harmonic rhythm. These arpeggios contain the expected modulation to vi (G minor), although there is no cadence. The arrival at V and the preparation for I bring this theme in the piano:

This is the second theme of the first ritornello, the one that was omitted in the first solo. Its reappearance later in a solo section was to be expected: Mozart's practice, however (in K. 450 and K. 453), was to bring it back in the third solo. J. C. Bach is witness to an interesting possibility of sonata style: the use of part of the exposition replayed *in the tonic* in order to prepare the return of the main theme at the tonic—in other words, part of what would be the recapitulation is displaced and used as the retransition.

This brings the second solo to a close. Third ritornello and third solo are combined, a practice that can be found many years earlier. The third solo, indeed, is traditionally the one with the most frequent interruptions from the orchestra. D. F. Tovey remarked that in Mozart the recapitulation of a concerto was a fusion of orchestral and solo expositions: and this principle begins to act long before Mozart. In J. C. Bach's third solo, one passage stands out, the reprise of the opening of the second group (see the original quoted at p. 91); it is handled with extraordinary finesse:

This displays the traditional move to the subdominant near the opening of the recapitulation, and also exploits the intimate relation between minor mode and subdominant, bringing out its latent expressive power with great skill.

The movement ends with a return of the opening bars. This proved to be another legacy of concerto technique to sonata style. Ending a symphony or sonata with first theme *forte* was too common a practice for me to cite examples: if the reader cannot remember any, he can amuse himself by looking—he will find them with ease. The appearance of a recapitulation in reverse order—that is, second group and the first theme only at the end—is a rare variant of this technique. We can find it occasionally in Haydn: there is a magnificent example in Mozart's Symphony in C major, K. 338, and an easily accessible one for pianists in the Piano Sonata in D major, K. 311, in which the order of recapitulation is: "second" theme, first two closing themes, opening theme, short coda, final closing theme. The "second theme" is clearly a solo, the main theme is in orchestral style, and the coda (see the example) is a burst of concerto-like virtuosity.

The relation of concerto to sonata is reciprocal. Sonata is less a form or set of forms than a way of conceiving and dramatizing the articulation of forms: concerto is a special kind of articulation. For some of the techniques of articulation, sonata style is directly indebted to the concerto. In turn, the articulations of concerto form are transformed by sonata style, ordered, balanced, and given new power.

VI ‮‬ Sonata Forms

THE METHOD OF ARTICULATING and dramatizing a variety of old forms that we call sonata style gave rise in turn to a new set of forms, equally various. If we order these forms according to the expressive intensity of the structures—that is, the importance of the tonic-dominant polarization, the degree to which this is heightened, the way the resolution is achieved—then we find that they fall broadly into four types, which correspond fairly well to whichever movement of the sonata as a whole employs them most frequently: first, second, minuet, or finale. First-movements forms are the most dramatically structured; those found most generally in finales—like the sonata-rondo, for example—are the most loosely organized, and the tonic-dominant polarity is eroded very early in the piece. Sonata-allegro or first-movement form may be employed anywhere, but the other forms are found, for the most part, in that movement of a sonata in which I classify them below, and very rarely in the opening one. These forms borrow from each other, and the characteristic patterns of one may shed light on another: finales, for example, illuminate the idea of recapitulation, as the stylistic conception of an ending is analogous in both. The following classification is intended not as a list of independent forms but as a spectrum.

1. First-Movement Sonata Form. This may be the most complex and tightly organized series of forms because of the tendency of the late eighteenth century to concentrate the greatest weight in the opening movement, which in consequence needed the most elaborate and most dramatic structure. This is the scheme which magnifies, beyond any other, the polarization of harmony, thematic material, and texture.

In first-movement form there are two sections. Either may be repeated, but the second is rarely repeated when the first is not. The opening bars establish a strict tempo, a tonic, characteristic thematic material, and texture as frames of reference. The polarization of tonic and dominant is created within these frames and enforced by discontinuity of texture (placing of cadences, changes of rhythm, dynamics), prolonged and then resolved.

To comprehend the structure of any individual movement, we must ask where the breaks in texture occur and how they are coordinated with the large-scale harmonic form and the thematic order. This is, somewhat more broadly put, the position of the eighteenth-century theorist: he asked largely where and how the cadences were placed. In the sonata, the cadences are reinforced by a brief pause, sudden changes of harmonic rhythm, or the appearance of a new theme. The thematic order is essentially an aspect of texture: the appearance of a new theme—or the reappearance of an old one—marks a clear break in texture when the theme has a clearly defined, memorable contour; the arrival of a theme enforces a structural point, makes an event, a moment of articulation. The coordination of harmony, texture, and thematic pattern defines each structural point dramatically as an interruption of the surface flow of the music. When the elements are out of phase, and they will often be so in the hands of a sophisticated composer, this is generally set in relief in sonata style so that the apparent lack of coordination is itself a dramatic effect—as when a Haydn recapitulation steals in at the middle of a phrase, or when Beethoven begins the recapitulation of opus 111 before the harmony has resolved to I:

The recapitulation begins here in the middle of the sequence at bar 90: the harmony is resolved only on the last beat of 91, and the theme is repeated at once to confirm the change.

In the first of the two sections of first-movement form (the exposition), there are three "events": the last event and one or both of the first two must be set in relief. They are:

a) the movement away from the tonic;
b) the establishment of the dominant (e.g., emphatic half-cadence on V of V);
c) confirmation of the modulation by a full cadence on V.

In early eighteenth-century works, the first two events are rarely emphasized by the texture, and the last is held back as far as possible until the end of the section: in the sonata, however, the half-cadence on V of V is succeeded by a theme, new or old, and a change in rhythmic movement.

Various ways of organizing an exposition were used in the eighteenth century, depending upon how and when the movement to V took place, and which aspects were to be set most into relief. When all three events were emphasized by breaks in texture, we have the standard nineteenth-century form, in which First Group, Bridge Passage, Second Group, and Concluding Theme are all clearly identifiable sections. This form is actually rare in the eighteenth century, as the move to the dominant is often initiated without a break from the statement or counterstatement, and the concluding theme may be a brief appendage to the second group: in this case, we have a two-part exposition:

A a) Statement of first group leading into the
    b) modulation ending with emphatic half-cadence.
B a) Second group, rounded off by
    b) emphatic cadential theme or themes.

Haydn, however, as J. P. Larsen has pointed out, often preferred a three-part organization. He arrives at this sometimes by a dramatic emphasis on the first and third events, and an absorption of the second into the flow of motivic development. This is particularly true of those movements called monothematic (although even there, he may make the reappearance of the first theme at the dominant a clear "event").

The exposition of Haydn's Symphony No. 44, the *Trauersymphonie* (pp. 101–105) provides a characteristic example of the three-part organization. The first group includes bars 1–19: the modulation to III is compressed into one bar at the very end in bar 19. The fierce and brilliant change of texture and harmony at bar 20 announces a new period. The first theme does not disappear, but it is given a counterpoint. This section goes to bar 42. The end of section 1 and the beginning of section 2

(*Text continues on p. 105*)

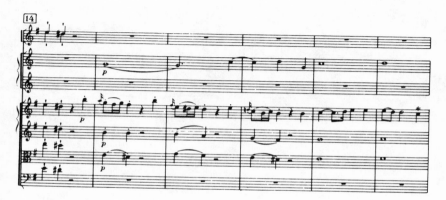

fuse both the movement away from the tonic and the arrival at the secondary tonality (III) into little more than a second of music.[1] This means that the new tonality must be established by weight: the second section is accordingly massive by contrast with the opening, and it is equally long. It confirms the new tonality by moving to its minor mode.

The third section also begins with the main theme, this time transformed into a cadential passage, with a full cadence in bar 53, repeated twice with the necessary conventional brilliance. These conventional formulas are absolutely essential to the form: they call attention only to what is fundamental here—the cadence. Bars 56 to 61 do not properly belong to the exposition: they are a transition back to the opening and also to the development that follows.

1. Note, however, the first horn in bar 17: its isolated F# (written D) stands out as a forewarning of something about to happen. Until then the horn has echoed the strings: now it moves to the leading tone of G, and sustains it for that split second (the third beat) when no other instrument plays, and prepares the modulation: probably no other contemporary composer exploited orchestration in this way.

I have quoted this example at length to show both how Haydn's unorthodox structures fulfill the expectations of the form as well as the more common procedures do, and how he uses one theme to the same purpose that another composer uses many. Mozart, for example, preferred to illustrate each of these events with a different motif and to round off each separate section of the exposition with yet another theme.

The second part of a sonata movement, Development/ Recapitulation, has at least two events: the return to the tonic and to some part of the material of the exposition in its original form, and a final confirming cadence on the tonic. We also often find an emphatic cadence on the relative minor at the end of the development before the retransition to I. The return to the tonic must generally take place about three-quarters of the way through the whole movement or before. The emphasis on the moment of return gives the length of the final section great importance. In general, the clarity of the periods in sonata style makes the proportions crucial. The longer the return to the tonic is postponed (i.e., the longer the development section), the greater the structural tension of the work, and consequently the greater the need for an extended resolution (i.e., recapitulation).

The tension is sustained harmonically, thematically and texturally: the harmony can move rapidly through dominant and subdominant key areas, establishing none of them for very long; the themes may be fragmented and combined in new ways and with new motifs; and the rhythm of the development section is in general more agitated, the periods less regular, the change of harmony more rapid and more frequent.

The resolution could not take place without the return of some part of the first half, and generally demands a replaying of all the important or memorable themes not already stated in the tonic. The thematic structure is, in the final analysis, not subordinate to harmony and texture in eighteenth-century sonata style (as is sometimes claimed today), but it does not dominate as it came to do very early in the nineteenth century.

Soon after the return to the tonic, there is often a *secondary development* section, which can be extensive, and almost always contains a reference to the subdominant: the "secondary development section" uses techniques of harmonic and motivic development not to prolong the tension of the exposition, but to reinforce the resolution on the tonic.

2. Slow-Movement Form. If there is no development section or merely a few transitional measures, the tension is minimized and a less dramatic structure results. (The secondary development section within the recapitulation may be retained.) In this form, which favors a more lyrical expression, there is generally a full cadence on the tonic at the end of the first group: the dominant is then simply introduced without modulation, and often confirmed only by a reference to its minor mode.

Any of the structural points which lend themselves to dramatization may often be passed over with very little fuss in this form. The return to the opening theme in the slow movement of Mozart's String Quartet in D major, K. 575, is as simple as possible; here is the last bar of A¹, the transition, and the first two bars of A²:

Perhaps because of his interest in the aria, Mozart made greater use of this form in instrumental music than other composers.[2]

The two sections of this form, A¹ and A² (exposition and recapitulation), are not repeated: the derivation of slow-movement form from the aria has been discussed above (see Chapter IV), and the two sections in the aria were originally one, slowly becoming binary only around 1720. The absence of one of the principal forces of dramatic tension, the prolonging of the polarization in the development section, makes this form most apt for slow movements, but Cimarosa used it for single-movement sonatas late in the century.

The form is also exceedingly common in opera overtures: excellent examples may be found in both *Idomeneo* and *The Marriage of Figaro* by Mozart, as well as in most of Rossini's overtures, Berlioz's *Waverly* overture, and elsewhere.

We should not confuse the retransition between exposition and recapitulation with a short development section. For example, the first movement of Mozart's great Piano and Violin Sonata in G major, K. 379, has an abnormally condensed but true development:

2. Besides K. 575, he employed it as well for the slow movements of the string quartets K. 387 in G major, K. 458 in Bb major, K. 465 in C major, and K. 589 in Bb major.

Here the development is reduced to a few bars, but it is nevertheless a first-movement form: it not only develops the closing theme (the motif in the piano) but admirably prolongs the harmonic tension. In addition, exposition and development/recapitulation are each repeated, and this distinguishes it from slow-movement form.

On the other hand, within a slow-movement form the secondary development section, which occurs soon after the beginning of the recapitulation, may gain in importance and keep the second part from being too literal a thematic reprise of the first. The function of the secondary development is, as I have said, to reaffirm the tonic by moving to a subdominant area,[3] but the motivic development may often be intensely dramatic. This secondary development, since it always modulates (however briefly) and touches upon subdominant keys, may use some of the material from the bridge, or from a modulating passage of the exposition, although this is by no means a general rule. In the slow movement of Mozart's Quartet in C major, K. 465 (The *Dissonance* Quartet), there is a remarkable expansion of the bridge by a secondary development. Here is the modulation from the tonic to dominant in the exposition:

3. See further below, pp. 289–96.

These thirteen bars (13–25) are enlarged to eighteen (57–74), and both the harmony and the melodic contour are made more poignant:

It is one of the most striking passages in the quartet. It begins by moving immediately to the subdominant and then to ii by bar 61: the chromaticism implies a return to F major through the minor mode. When it is elaborate, as here, the secondary development produces a second return to the tonic in the recapitulation, or at least the illusion of a return—it creates a harmonic event where there would otherwise be only a working-out of a thematic pattern in a single tonality. In this way, the reappearance of the second theme is set in relief just as it was in the exposition.

There are several examples of slow-movement form in Haydn's quartets: the third movements of opus 9 no. 3, of 1769; opus 17 no. 3, of 1771; opus 17 no. 5, with a wonderful recitative passage in both A¹ and A² as a second group between first and closing themes; opus 33 no. 3, of 1781; and a beautiful example from 1797, the second movement of opus

76 no. 4, in which the recapitulation begins in the tonic minor (an almost obsolete device by then). This whole section is so reconceived as to provide an extraordinary thematic development in a harmonic structure that clearly resolves—a secondary development with its bias towards the subdominant:

The end of the exposition is bar 30, followed by four bars of retransition to the tonic: what comes after never leaves the key of Eb, and from bar 43 on it is the major mode that governs.

Haydn also uses slow-movement form in the movement called "A Dream" in Quartet op. 50 no. 5 of 1785, and in op. 50 no. 2 as well. Beethoven uses it, among other places, for the second movement of Symphony no. 4, and most strikingly for the second movement (not a slow movement) of the Quartet in C♯ minor, op. 131.

Mozart uses slow-movement form with alternating tempi in two violin sonatas (K. 303 and K. 306, both of 1778). Here we find the form exceptionally in the first movement, justified by the dramatic changes of tempi. The tonal plan of K. 303 is:

Adagio	Molto Allegro	Adagio	Molto Allegro
I——→V	V	I	I

the first adagio ending with a half-cadence on V of V. This scheme of alternating tempi is derived from opera buffa.

A variant of slow-movement form may be called the rondo-slow-movement form. It can be found in the third movement of Haydn's Quartet op. 33 no. 4, in Bb major, of 1781, and in the second movement of Mozart's Sonata for Piano in D major, K. 311, of 1777. In this variant form the first theme returns at the end:

A	B	A	B	A
I	V	I	I	I

The main characteristic of all examples and variants of slow-movement form is in fact shared with the rondo: the immediate turn to resolution at the end of the exposition.

3. Minuet Sonata Form is in two parts but in three (large) phrases or periods: phrases two and three go together. In other words, the double bar is placed at the end of the first phrase, which may have a cadence either on the tonic or the dominant. The second phrase either establishes or extends the dominant, develops it very briefly, and turns back to the tonic. The third phrase begins in the tonic and resolves or recapitulates. When the form is enlarged and the first phrase is expanded at great length, as it is very late in the century, this pattern merges quickly with first-movement form. The retransition from phrases two to three may be given to a short intermediate phrase, but the three-period structure is always absolutely clear. It may be expanded by a coda or by interior echoes, but the relation of these to the basic three-period structure is not often in doubt. (Minuets in two phrases are sometimes used as trios, but they are rare otherwise: the minuet in Beethoven's Piano Sonata, op. 31 no. 3 is one such exception.)

Beethoven, who expanded the minuet form beyond the range of any other composer, continued to write the simplest and plainest examples. Here is the *Alla danza tedesca* from opus 130, which I quote in order to show this form in its purest state:

The minuet sonata is conservative, its derivation from three-phrase binary form of the early eighteenth century obvious. The three phrases do not have to be exactly equal (although they often are), but they must balance each other, their contours defined without equivocation. In spite of the conservative, even reactionary, aspect of this form, it must be classed with the sonata forms because the relations of the three periods to each other are, at least by the 1770s, conceived in terms of sonata style. It is, however, the shortest of all these sonata forms, as well as the most stereotyped, and it is useful as a comparison: within a miniature form certain stylistic details which cannot be reduced as much as the whole form stand out in high relief.

The relative brevity of most minuets also explains an anomaly—or what ought to be an anomaly: the fact that it makes so little difference whether the first period has a cadence on I or on V. The form is strictly binary, and the first period stands alone before the double bar and is repeated; periods two and three together form the second unit, repeated in turn. If the harmonic structure is as important as we suspect it to be for the eighteenth century, then the cadence of the first part of a binary form ought to count for a great deal.

The first period of a minuet may have a cadence on I, a weak cadence on V (still in the tonic), or a strong cadence on V (after a modulation to the dominant). In the minuets of the last six symphonies of Haydn, for example, the first period in nos. 99, 101, and 102 closes with a modulation to V, in no. 103 with a half-cadence on V, and in nos. 100 and 104 with a strong cadence on the tonic. First periods with a modulation to V are longer and somewhat more elaborate than others, but this changes neither the character nor the relative proportions of the form in any remarkable way. The reason lies in the large scale of modulation in sonata style and the brevity of the minuet: the first period alone may be long enough both to define the tonic and to make a modulation, but not long enoug'. to confirm the opposition of tonalities, or to give this opposition sufficient solidity and mass to make it of any consequence. That task is therefore left to the second period.

This is the essence of minuet sonata form, and its interest lies exactly in this odd attribute: the second period, after the double bar and always linked to the third period, generally creates some of the polarity of tonic and dominant necessary to the late eighteenth-century composer, or it produces subsidiary modulations that increase the tension of the move away from the tonic; it may act like a Second Group, or like a development section, or even like both at once. In first-movement form, the modulation of the exposition is given its power by the length of the second group, while the harmonic changes of the development, however surprising and far-flung, have none of that solidity. In minuet form, the harmonic movement of the second period (after the double bar) has often a much greater force than whatever has preceded it.

If the first period ends on I, the second will most likely move to V and prepare the return to I. If the first period ends on V, the second will either continue it or make a leap to a remote key area. In either case the principal effect of opposition is created *over* the double-bar line.

The *Menuetto* of Haydn's Quartet in C major, op. 74 no. 1, plays a witty joke with the cadence of the first period: Haydn pretends to go to I, and then suddenly swerves off to V. After a regular eight-bar phrase with cadence on I, the move to V is sudden and harmonically flimsy; it gains conviction only by the repeated accented syncopations:

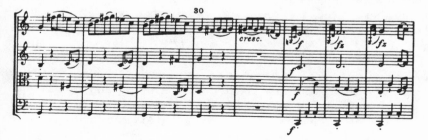

The second period moves boldly to the remote A♭ and starts a sequential development section that turns back to the tonic. The third period, or recapitulation, starts at bar 32 and demonstrates how the small-scale structural detail stands out in so brief a form. At bar 40, we reach the point of the recapitulation where the exposition swerved off to V: here Haydn has placed the secondary development section, the move through the subdominant region back to the tonic. In so short a movement (period one: 14 bars; period two: 17 bars), this takes so large a place (6 bars), that almost a full second return is demanded. It starts accordingly in bar 49. This expands the third period considerably, making it exactly twice as long as the first. The technique and the placing of the expansion are not essentially different from those used in first-movement form, but the relation of exposition to recapitulation is heard at once when the two periods are so short.

The second and third periods in Haydn's minuets are often enlarged by codas, generally tacked on with little pretense at continuity. The periods are clearly defined, and we know when each one is over: echoes and codas are obviously extra. This is a source of the sublime wit in the trio of the minuet of Symphony no. 85: the coda of the second period is not only too long (the coda is twice as long as the period itself!) but much too long—it is there just to make us wait:

Menuetto D.C.

The coda is, of course, a retransition—not that one was really needed: it is delightful because it is so absurdly gratuitous. This is pure sonata style; the significance comes from the technique of articulation, the play with structure.

An expansion of minuet form of a very different nature is placed in the trio of the minuet from Haydn's *Emperor* Quartet, op. 76 no. 3:

The expansion is a simple insertion. Period 2 goes from bars 9 to 20, period 3 from 37 to the end (bar 44). Between them (bars 21 to 36) is a simple binary form in the major mode, two almost perfectly symmetrical phrases, with a half-cadence on V replaced by I, the second phrase enriched by imitation. At the end of the insertion, the third period takes up the opening phrase of the trio as if nothing had happened. The absolute simplicity disguises the fact that this is one of the most sophisticated structures in all eighteenth-century chamber music. The magical quality of the major mode in that wonderful insertion is due in part to its being extraneous to the form—it is unprepared (except by the mysterious fermata at the end of period 2) and it has no effect on the form, which continues as if those bars had never existed: one could go from bar 20 to 37 and never know that something had been omitted. The two little phrases in the major mode could only have been inserted at this point, but they do not alter the structure: Haydn uses the contrast of major and minor as pure expression. That is why it sounds like Schubert, who was to rediscover in his songs the purely expressive nonstructural alternation of major and minor modes—and then went on in the great G-major Quartet to make of this alternation the principal structural element of a sonata form.

More than any other type of movement, minuets (and scherzos) demonstrate that the evolution of sonata forms was not the development of a single model, but the transformation of several earlier formal patterns. Retaining its dance character even when it was called scherzo, the minuet was consequently the most recalcitrant of these early forms, the most resistant to transformation. For a long time—well into the late nineteenth century—the opening section before the first double bar tended to be a single period, with no second theme or second group, and no decisive polarization of tonic and dominant; often there is only a simple half-cadence on the dominant or even a tonic cadence, and this opening section only rarely resembles the "exposition" of what was later to become the standard sonata form. However, what followed this opening period generally exhibited, from a very early date, some of the characteristics of "sonata": thematic development in the second period, with fragmentation of the themes, chromatic and sequential harmonies, and an elaborate preparation for the decisive return of the tonic and the opening bars. We frequently find the same techniques and the same stereotypes in the second half of minuets that we find in other movements, although in minuets they tend to appear on a more modest scale. It would be absurd to ascribe these traits to an influence from a then non-existent standard first-movement form, as the characteristics of sonata appear as early in minuets as they do in other binary forms. Just as what we have called "slow-movement" form (or "overture" or "cavatina" form) is not a first-movement form with the development omitted but the reworking of an earlier and independent pattern, so minuet sonata form is a dramatization and enlargement of an already existing form, made more effective, more public.

What is instructive is that the earlier pattern remains clearly visible under the transformation; this did not prevent composers from using the same advanced techniques at vital structural points that they employed in other movements. The minuet of Mozart's "Jupiter" Symphony, K. 551, for example, after the first double bar has a sequential development of the opening motif and a dramatic preparation of the return of the theme: in addition, like the famous finale, there is a coda with complex four-voice imitative counterpoint and a ritornello-like return of a passage that followed the opening bars. The trio of this same minuet has a second period that ends with the half cadence on the dominant of the relative minor (V of vi) that we find in so many first movements[4] and an ingenious transition:

4. See pages 267–72 for a discussion of this stereotype.

This is pure sonata technique. The scherzo of Beethoven's "Eroica" Symphony has a simple first period of fourteen bars that is repeated unaltered except for changes of instrumentation. The return, however, has a full dramatic sonata articulation, with a half-cadence of V of iii substituted for V of vi after a contrapuntal development

and this is succeeded by a powerful return of the main theme played fortissimo by the full orchestra. It is clear that we do not have to start with a full exposition to arrive at the elements of sonata form, although when the exposition is missing we must expect the second half of the movement to do some of its work. These examples demonstrate that sonata is not strictly a form or even a range of forms—although we have found it convenient to describe it as such—but a way of articulating and transforming a set of forms inherited from the early eighteenth century.

4. **Finale Sonata Form** is more loosely organized, and tends by its very looseness to a resolution of tension. What is essential is a squareness and clarity of rhythm and phrasing, and generally an emphasis on the subdominant as well as a broad use of the tonic equivalent to the similar emphasis in a recapitulation. If we compare the open-

ings of the first and last movements of Beethoven's Fifth Symphony, we have a model of the difference in phrasing and the emphasis on the tonic that were necessary for the firm sense of ending indispensible in a finale. As in slow-movement form, the first theme is generally rounded off by a full cadence on the tonic, and does not move directly into a modulation. The square phrase structure which isolates each theme is especially suitable for rondo form.

Rondos are defined as much by the characters of their themes as by the structure. Technically a sonata rondo is merely a first-movement form in which the theme is completely restated between second group and development section and yet again at the end:

A	B	A	C	A	B	A
I	V	I	Dev.	I	I	I

But not every theme can take this kind of treatment. A rondo theme is generally a complete form in itself, either a two-phrase binary form as in the Rondo from Mozart's Piano Sonata, K.309:

RONDEAU
Allegretto grazioso

or a ternary form as in the last movement of Beethoven's Opus 90:

Nicht zu geschwind und sehr singbar vorgetragen

The rondo theme is not only complete in itself, but within the theme the individual elements are isolated and constantly repeated.

The two halves of Mozart's theme are identical for several bars except for the addition of an intensifying ornament, and the first three bars of Beethoven's are played without change (except a shift of register and a little variation at the end, bars 28–29) four times within the theme—indeed, the complete theme reappears four times in the movement, and the opening bars are repeated for the last time towards the end. We have ample time to get acquainted with the melody: the rondo is evidently a leisurely form even when the tempo is quick. (It would seem, paradoxically, that melodies with the greatest amount of interior repetition lend themselves most easily to being repeated without change and without development.) The emphasis on the tonic in Beethoven's theme is remarkable: there are tonic cadences at the ends of most of the phrases (bars 4, 8, 16, 24, 28, and 32), and the other points of the periodic four-bar phrasing land on IV (bars 12 and 20). This concentration on tonic and subdominant is a feature both of recapitulation and of the finale in general.

The relation of the classical sonata rondo to Philip Emanuel Bach's rondos (essentially modulating fantasias, with the main theme reappearing in different keys) is too complex to enter into here. The derivation from the early eighteenth-century rondeau (basically an extension of ternary form ABACA) is obvious enough. A few points about sonata rondo, however, have to be made which will help to understand the finale in the late eighteenth century.

There is a form of rondo which must be classed as sonata rondo although there is no development. The rondo by Mozart quoted above (p. 124), is in such a form. It has many themes, and I label each one with a letter:

Exposition		Return of theme	Subdominant episode		Recapitulation reversed	Coda
A B C D E F		A	D G		C D E A F	C B A
I I—→V V V V		I	I—→ IV IV		I I I I I	I I I

The scheme only looks complicated because Mozart uses so many themes: it is very simple in practice. The Mozart rondo generally has a recapitulation in reverse—playing the second group first, then the first theme, and then the closing theme. The form of K. 309 is an exposition and reverse recapitulation framing a return of the main theme and a new episode at the subdominant.

This form may be combined with a development section, and the finale of the G-minor Viola Quintet, K. 516, does so:

Exposition	Return	Subdominant/Development episode	Recapitulation reversed
A B C D I I V V	A I	E IV	C D A B I I I I

There are two completely separate and elaborate themes in the first group, only the first of which returns after the exposition. The exposition from the early eighteenth-century rondeau (basically an extension in reverse order.

The sonata rondo is therefore not a fixed form for Mozart: it may have a development section, or a subdominant episode, or both—or neither: the finale of the Sinfonia Concertante for Violin and Viola, K. 364, of 1779 is clearly a rondo in character with no development and no central episode in subdominant or in any other key, but the recapitulation does begin in the subdominant.

These elements are ordered in still another way in the finale of the Viola Quintet in C major, K. 515. This, too, is clearly a rondo, with a square-cut theme that reappears often throughout the movement. The form approximates slow-movement or aria-sonata form. I give the parallels between the exposition and the recapitulation:

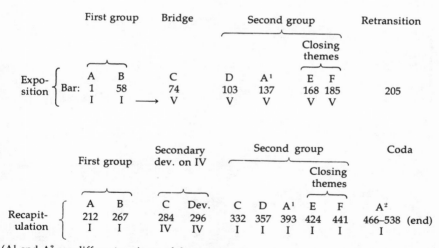

		First group		Bridge	Second group		Closing themes		Retransition
Expo- sition	Bar:	A 1 I	B 58 I	C 74 $\longrightarrow$ V	D 103 V	A¹ 137 V	E 168 V	F 185 V	205

		First group		Secondary dev. on IV		Second group			Closing themes		Coda
Recapit- ulation		A 212 I	B 267 I	C 284 IV	Dev. 296 IV	C 332 I	D 357 I	A¹ 393 I	E 424 I	F 441 I	A² 466–538 (end) I

(A¹ and A² are different variants of the opening theme.)

The development section, which is wonderfully elaborate, is placed where a secondary development would be in first-movement or slow-movement form, and it has the harmonic character of the secondary de-

velopment in a recapitulation, moving through the subdominant back to
the tonic:

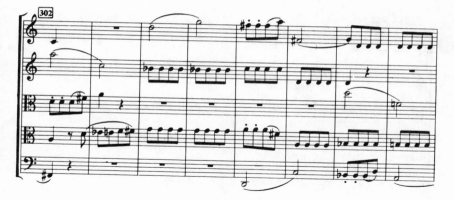

The style of the movement is, however, that of a rondo and the variant A¹ of the main theme that appears in the second group is very similar to the main theme itself. To analyze the structure as a traditional sonata rondo would only obscure how the development functions in the movement as a whole. It moves from the tonic through the subdominant area back to the tonic and works exactly like the passages of development often found in recapitulations. Analyzing it as a slow-movement form reveals this most easily, and we have remarked above on a similar use of this form in rondo style for the finale of the Quartet in E♭ major, K. 428.

It is against this background that we can understand the famous repeat in the last movement of Beethoven's *Appassionata*, op. 57, which seems to have puzzled so many critics as well as pianists. It is only the *second* half of what appears to be a regular first-movement form that is repeated. This second half, however, starts with the principal theme played in the subdominant and a new theme in the subdominant follows. This is the familiar subdominant episode of a rondo finale. The repetition of the second part enhances the rondo character of the form by emphasizing, not the tonic-dominant opposition, but the subdominant and repetition of the main theme.

These individual examples may help to explain why the textbook sonata rondo finally came into being. What counted in the finale was the large size of the tonic areas, the emphasis on the subdominant, and the generally loose episodic construction—all this was in keeping with a sonata aesthetic. Some of the most characteristic elements of the sonata rondo—the rounded symmetrical main theme with a full cadence on the tonic, the emphasis on the subdominant (often with a theme that appears only in that area), the loosely articulated construction with the joints clearly marked—appear frequently in finales that are not in rondo form. The central subdominant episode is a good example: a new theme in the subdominant is found in the middle of the finales of Mozart's Quartet in A major, K. 464, and Piano Sonata in F major, K. 332, neither of which are rondos. Here is the episode of K. 332:

The reappearance of the scherzo in the finale of Beethoven's Symphony no. 5 is a sophisticated example of this phenomenon (the tonic minor is in the subdominant area[4] and is used in the center of rondo finales as well, e.g., Mozart's Violin Concerto in A major).

The finale of Haydn's Piano Trio in A♭ major of 1785 (H.XV:14) is called a rondo by the composer himself. It has, indeed, a theme of rondo character and takes the following shape:

```
A (dev.) A B  ‖: Dev. A Dev. A (dev.) A B
I ⟶ V V  :‖  vi IV vi I      I I
```

This is, of course, first-movement form in Haydn's monothematic style, with a long section on IV in the development. It is however, properly termed a rondo even if it does not answer the descriptions of the form generally given. It sounds like a rondo. The sonata rondo is therefore an idiosyncratic version of finale-sonata form, perhaps the most efficient of the patterns evolved to that end. It is not the result of blending two independent preexisting forms, but the stylistic inflection and transformation of one preexistant form, the rondo, remarkable for the aptness with which it fulfilled the late eighteenth century's requirements for a concluding movement.

4. The subdominant character of the tonic minor may appear puzzling, but a movement to the tonic minor is a movement in the flat direction of the diatonic circle of fifths. Since in equal temperament flat and sharp directions are, at the limit, transformed into each other, much depends on how a given modulation is prepared and established. Nevertheless, a simple jump from tonic major to tonic minor has clearly more in common with a jump to the subdominant than to the dominant: a quick move to tonic minor or subdominant implies neither increase in tension nor polarity, but simple contrast with a neighboring area. This is why the tonic minor can substitute for the more standard subdominant in rondo forms.

The central subdominant episode functions like a central trio, the middle part of an ABA form, and this reminds us of the frequency of the minuet finale in the second half of the eighteenth century, above all in the piano concerto (those of J. C. Bach, for example), the violin sonata (of Schobert and Mozart), and the piano trio of Haydn. After 1780, a ternary form is often completely transformed and dramatized by sonata style: Haydn liked to give the middle section of his free ternary forms the character of a development section with a climax and a retransition—and often this does not suffice, and a second development is added as a coda. By this means Haydn gave a ternary form enough dramatic force to serve exceptionally as a first movement, (for example, the Quartet in D major, op. 76 no. 5), and endowed the minuet finales of the last piano trios with such extraordinary weight.

VII [*]   Evolution of Sonata Forms

THE SONATA FORMS—with their fundamental discontinuities, polarities, and clearly defined, independent periods—required a renunciation of the High Baroque conception of continuity, an escape from its *horror vacui*. The Germans, masters of the contrapuntal technique long associated with church music, and the French, tied to court and operatic traditions of a certain stately decorum, were not well prepared for such a radical change. It came at first more easily to the Italians. By the 1730s, in the works of Giovanni Battista Sammartini, Domenico Scarlatti and others, the break with Baroque texture is manifest. The single phrases are independent, their proportions clearly defined.

In the works of both composers, but used with special effectiveness by Scarlatti, we find the same means of overriding the breaks in texture and restoring a continuity, but a continuity of a new kind that no longer demanded a homogeneous texture: the arrangement of the phrases in symmetrical periods—at this time two-measure phrases above all, although groups of three- and four-measure phrases are also found. (Not until the nineteenth century did the four- and eight-measure periodic rhythm become tyrannical: throughout the eighteenth century, the construction remained admirably supple.) A periodic grouping superimposes a slow but dynamic beat over the inner beats of the bar: as a means of generating movement in sonata style, the period replaced the harmonic sequences of the Baroque, although in the 1730s it was still generally accompanied by sequential movement.

In Scarlatti, too, the Baroque drift from the tonic to the dominant is often replaced by a violent opposition of tonalities. The first half of Sonata K. 140 shows this at its most striking:

133

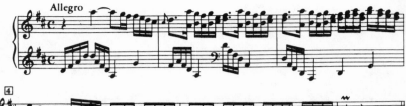

The move from I to V is accomplished dramatically by an astonishing juxtaposition of the tonic, D, and the key of the flatted leading tone, C (bar 7). This is a very sophisticated procedure, anticipating in its powerful simplicity some of the effects of late Haydn. But it is also an example of a common practice of early sonata style: it enables Scarlatti to approach the dominant by means of its minor mode. This direction and resolution of the D major/C major clash, however, shows that Scarlatti has a command of the whole spectrum of tonalities that we find nowhere else in the 1740s. (It is interesting that, although the minor mode appears to last until the end of the section, the last unharmonized note must be understood as major. It leads directly back to the opening D major, so that one accepts the unharmonized A as an implied V. This is confirmed when the second part starts at once in A major.) An interesting aspect of this sonata is its obvious imitation of orchestral textures.

It should not be concluded, however, that the sonata forms were created in Italy, but only that some of the prerequisite elements of sonata style appeared at an early date in Italy and Spain (where Domenico Scarlatti composed almost his entire keyboard *oeuvre*). Scarlatti's structures can still largely be subsumed under the category of binary form. In the second half of most of his sonatas, the point of return to the tonic is not clearly articulated. In some, the opening bars do return at the tonic, but the moment generally passes without any attempt to call attention to it. Here is the opening of K.212 in A major:

And here, buried in a D-minor/D-major passage (note the change of key signature), is the return:

This is magnificent, of course, but it is not sonata form and none the worse for that. Very occasionally, Scarlatti attempts something like a slow-movement or aria-sonata form and begins the second part with a return to bar 3 of the opening. K.218, for example, begins:

and the second part commences by taking these bars up again:

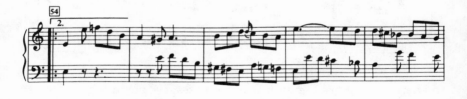

continuing like the second part (A²) of the aria of the 1740s by a turn to the subdominant and a return to I.

As for the rare sonata by Scarlatti where the return to the tonic in the second half is set in relief, we usually find that in the first half the modulation to the dominant has been marked by no discontinuity and that there has been no strong cadence until the double bar; the polarization has not been made explicit so that the return does not have the full significance it would have in sonata form.

The elements of sonata style appear at first in isolation. It is easy to attach too much importance to these isolated appearances. An articulated recapitulation has none of the meaning it will have for sonata style when it has not been preceded by an articulated exposition that demands resolution. The very few works of the 1730s which conform closely to the later model have no special weight; to single them out is to distort their significance. The rare sonatas of Scarlatti, for example, that begin the recapitulation with the opening theme are not in a form essentially different from the others; to label them as precursors of a later "Classical" style is anachronistic. They represent only one of the stylistic possibilities of the time in which they were created.

The symphonies of Giovanni Battista Sammartini have a similarly ambiguous but important historical relation to the mature sonata forms. His early symphonies[1] are generally in three-phrase binary form, and the return to the tonic is almost always marked by a return to the opening material. There is also a progressive avant-garde taste for contrasting textures. These, however, are not well coordinated with the harmonic structure, as Sammartini was not skilled at handling harmonic movement. Here is the exposition of a Symphony in A major (labelled no. 15 by Churgin and Jenkins):

1. Edited by Bathia Churgin, Cambridge, Mass., 1968.

The opening theme is elegantly characterized, above all, by the contrast of texture and line in bars 5–9. The problems begin with the voice-leading of bars 12 and 13 and the handling of the modulation to V: after a return to the tonic and then even the subdominant (in bar 15), the attempt to move back to V has been hopelessly enfeebled. Sammartini appeared to think that if he sat on the dominant long enough (from bars 17 to 20), the listener would be convinced by the following cadence (bars 22–23). Bar 26 tries to right matters, but by then it is too late.

We must expect a composer working in a new style to lose his grip of some of the fundamental elements of an old one. If we wish to see how an older and more reactionary contemporary of Sammartini achieved a convincing move from I to V, we may take the first solo and beginning of the second ritornello of the *Italian Concerto:*

This gives a lesson in classical modulation without resort to any contrast of texture: the emphasis on the dominant, then the reference to V of V (G-major triad), the glance at V of V of V (D major), and the slight

suggestion of v (C minor) before affirming the arrival at C major. Then
Bach throws it all away by moving to IV (Bb major) at the end of the second phrase of the ritornello: he is not interested in the polarization of I
and V which he has in fact established. Those of his contemporaries
who were interested lacked his mastery. The sonata does not exist until
this harmonic sense was recovered and combined with the more up-to-
date feeling for texture and periodic rhythm.

There are, indeed, expositions of Sammartini where the polarization of I and V is established more convincingly, and which have an interesting sense of contrast of textures to enforce it. The Symphony in F
major, no. 6, shows this.

The crucial bars are 6 to 8 and they work—at the expense of an unbelievably ugly melodic line for Violin I. (We must be thankful that the tempo is presto.) It is easy to see why Haydn called Sammartini a *Schmierer;* nevertheless, he showed the way the wind was blowing in the 1730s and 1740s.

Several of the works he wrote at this time have a "development section" of a special kind. They are to be played piano with a reduced orchestra by contrast with the unvaried forte of the exposition and recapitulation. Here are the first bars of the exposition and the "development" of the Symphony in A major (no. 16):

In the first eight measures of the "development" the opening theme is played at the dominant, a trait of Baroque binary form that was never to be entirely abandoned as a possibility by the sonata: then, in the tonic minor, comes the long passage marked piano for reduced orchestra. These characteristics—reduced dynamics and thinner texture (removal of the double basses), and the tonic minor—are those of the central section of an ABA ternary form, above all that of the aria. This "development" does not yet realize the relationship of a sonata development to the exposition. It is a short two-phrase binary form, which provides the expressive but less powerful contrast of a trio in a minuet or aria. It is, therefore, the middle part of a ternary construction comfortably ensconced between two halves of a binary form. Both binary and ternary forms have been eroded and weakenened until a loose synthesis begins to be possible. We have already seen examples of a trio placed between an exposition and a recapitulation in the opera aria, and we shall have to return briefly to this form once again. It is interesting, nevertheless, how these works of the 1730s show the significant emergence of isolated elements of sonata style from the forms of a previous tradition.

Other elements of the style come from the German composers, who lag only a few years behind the Italians in exploiting the new taste for simplicity, clarity, and independently defined periodic structure. Hermann Abert noted the existence of two separate German approaches to the sonata forms: a North German tradition, which favored thematic unity in order to achieve a unity of sentiment in each movement; and the Viennese tradition, which sought for affective contrast and a rich variety of thematic material. These two traditions come together quickly in the late 1750s, above all in the music of Haydn where a synthesis is effected.

The most prominent representative of the North German tradition was Philip Emanuel Bach, a composer whose interest in intimate and intense expression led him to explore the possibilities of dissonance and remote key relationships (i.e., dissonance on a higher structural level). Striking modulations in Scarlatti are generally more coloristic than expressive; in C. P. E. Bach, they have a remarkable and sometimes incoherent passion which is reflected in the intense and idiosyncratic character of his themes. The highly individualized motif or theme was to become central to sonata style.

In most composers of the 1730s and 1740s, like Domenico Alberti, Sammartini and Johann Stamitz, such thematic individuality is minimal. This individuality is found frequently in Scarlatti, but it is there usually unrelated to the large formal design of the work. C. P. E. Bach's treatment of the striking and memorable motif, however, was crucial for the history of the sonata forms. Unity of theme and unity of sentiment were almost synonymous for the North German school. The theme had not only to be immediately expressive, but capable of conveying by itself the developing formal significance from polarization to resolution demanded by sonata style. In other words, the themes of C. P. E. Bach are capable of transformation, of "development," and remain sufficiently memorable for their identity to be clear through the transformations. Both the strikingly individual motif and development by transformation and fragmentation exist in Baroque style, but it was C. P. E. Bach above all who made them available for sonata style and showed how they could be used in the creation of forms.

The South German, or Viennese, tradition is a more amiable one: for the composers of this school, of whom the most important is Wagenseil, the forms were created with a variety of themes, many of them of a frankly popular character. This richness of material is not restricted to the expositions, and the practice of initiating the development section with a new theme (a device that continued to be employed by Mozart and later composers) is already in evidence in the Viennese tradition by the early 1750s. This practice derives as we have seen from late Baroque concerto form, where the second solo section began traditionally with a relatively free development of new material.

It is important to emphasize the variety of sonata patterns available to composers in the 1750s—indeed they remained available until the nineteenth century, when the choice becomes more restricted, and the original freedom reappears only in the late work of Beethoven. The keyboard sonatas of Giovanni Marco (Placido) Rutini published in 1757 show this variety. I deliberately choose one set of sonatas to demonstrate how many different forms are present at a given moment. In the six sonatas grouped as opus 3, we find recapitulations, for example, conceived in the following ways:

1) Full recapitulation of the exposition after a development section ending on vi (Sonata no. V, mvt. 3). This is the standard sonata recapitulation of the nineteenth century.

2) Full recapitulation of first group and of one of the two themes of the second group after a development, part of which was devoted to the other principal theme of the second group, played in the relative minor (Sonata no. VI, mvt. 1).

3) Full recapitulation of the exposition beginning on the subdominant, a form that was to become a lazy mannerism only after 1800 (Sonata no. IV, mvt. 1).

4) Recapitulation in the mid-century symphonic style, beginning with the third bar of the exposition, here starting on the subdominant (Sonata no. III, mvt. 2).

5) Recapitulation in the older style of the binary dance form, i.e., only of the second group, but with the arrival at the tonic well in relief (Sonata no. I, mvt. 2 and Sonata no. II, mvt. 1).

6) Recapitulation only of second group with no articulation of the arrival at I (Sonata no. II, mvt. 2). This is, of course, the most reactionary form.

Most of the formal possibilities that sonata form will develop are, as we can see, already present in the 1750s. All of these patterns coexist comfortably, the nineteenth-century textbook form along side of the old-fashioned Baroque form. And they continue to coexist throughout the eighteenth century, their powers of endurance creating no stylistic problem. In 1791, an English admirer of Haydn, Christian Latrobe, published three piano sonatas;[2] Haydn accepted the dedication. We find in these works the following kinds of recapitulation:

Sonata I, mvt. 1. Reactionary. Reprise only of second group.
            2. Full recapitulation, freely reworked.
            4. "Cyclical" or "Romantic" form. Reappearance of the main theme of the first movement at the end of the finale!

Sonata II, mvt. 1. Recapitulation in reverse, first group appearing only at the end.

Sonata III, mvt. 2. Recapitulation with the mid-century symphonic stereotype, beginning only with the third bar of the main theme. The opening bars return later, as they do in the exposition.

In spite of his admiration for Haydn, Latrobe clings to old patterns that Haydn had more or less abandoned by the 1780s: he is also well up on the latest forms and even somewhat in advance of them. He may have been showing off in using so many different forms, but so much the better: the history of music ought to be concerned with the *range* of forms and styles available at any given moment.

The cyclical return of the first movement in the finale of Sonata no. I in A major has much historical charm, above all because this exceedingly modern effect is achieved with the most conventional eighteenth-century material. Here is the beginning of the first movement, and a later version of the motif as well:

2. Edited by Charles E. Stevens, New York, 1970.

And here is the last part of Latrobe's short presto finale:

The quick tempo gives this Romantic prefiguration a disarmingly unpretentious naïveté.

To return briefly to Rutini's opus 3 and the great variety of sonata patterns available to a composer at mid century: the opening of the second half of the sonata (the beginning of the "development section") offered a wide range of possibilities, comparable to the opening of the recapitulation. The device most frequently found—and it remained the most popular form for many decades—was that of starting the development with the main theme at the dominant. Other choices were open, however. Sonata no. I in D major starts the development section of its principal movement (the second, since the first movement is a prelude in an improvisatory style) with new material arranged sequentially, followed by the main theme at the dominant. I give the opening theme, and then the first dozen bars or so of the "development":

This device of opening the development section with new material is, as we have seen, probably inherited from concerto form.

Two other patterns, both found in Sonata no. III in C major, play an important role in the history of eighteenth-century style. One is the return of the main theme only at the third bar after a brief development based on the theme. We see this in the first movement; once again I give the main theme, and the opening of the second part:

This is what I have called type 3 of the basic aria form: A^2 begins with a statement of the main theme at the dominant or a development of it through the supertonic (as here, starting with dominant minor), the tonic entering to take up the thematic pattern where it broke off, moving at once to IV.

The last movement presents a related form: the second part begins with the opening theme at V, immediately repeated at I. Here is the main theme, and the opening of the second part:

This is an example of type 2 of the aria form (and once again the move to IV occurs without delay). In instrumental music, Oliver Strunk has called this "premature reprise"[3]. It is, of course, only premature if you think it happens too soon. We shall return briefly to this; the richness and variety of sonata forms at mid-century is our concern here.

Haydn's work in the 1750s and later reveals the same richness. An example of this early freedom may be seen in the Quartet op. 2 no. 2 in E, which dates from the late '50s. The exposition of the first movement has four themes: A and B in the tonic, and A¹ (a variation of A) and C in the dominant. Here is the exposition:

3. See below, p. 155ff and reference.

The two themes of the first group are very regular: eight bars each, the second moving to V in bars 15–16. The theme at bars 17–28, which begins the second group and establishes V more solidly, is just a variation of the first eight bars. The new theme at bar 29 has again many elements in common with the opening but presents an individual contour. Each variant of the main motifs is clearly recognizable.

Let us look now at the order of themes in the recapitulation:

The order of themes has now become A A¹ C B—reasonably, since A¹ was used in the exposition as the beginning of the second group to affirm the dominant. Here, where everything must remain in the tonic, the main interest of A¹ will be its derivation from A, and they are accordingly played one after the other. The theme we have labelled B, on the other hand, is the jolliest tune in the piece, and it is effectively displaced to the end, closing the movement in a popular vein.

Naturally such freedom would come easily when there was no such thing as "sonata form." In the opening movement of Haydn's Quartet in F major, op. 2 no. 4, the principal theme reappears in the middle of the development section in the subdominant, a *false reprise* which turns out to be a real one as the theme never appears again, and the tonic finally reenters with a later motif from the first group.

The dominance of the standard form is generally dated too early. James Webster, in the *New Grove*, writes that "its unchallenged reign in instrumental art music did not begin until about 1770." *The New Harvard Dictionary of Music* claims: "By about 1765, however, full sonata form—though never the rigid textbook variety—was rapidly becoming the norm in fast movements." For both works of reference, the full form implies a return to the tonic with the opening theme in the second part after a development section.

Johann Christian Bach published two sets of six sonatas: opus 5 in 1766, and opus 17 in 1774. In how many first movements do we find "full sonata form"? Opus 5 no. 5 in E major recapitulates only the second group, and starts that in the relative minor. In no. 3 in G major the main theme never reappears at the tonic, nor does it in no. 6 in C minor, which begins with a slow binary introduction to a fugue, neither part repeated (the second movement is a gavotte). In opus 17, neither no. 3 in E♭ nor no. 6 in B♭ have a recapitulation of the first group; no. 5 in A starts to recapitulate the first theme in bar 5 of the second part after some arpeggios, drops it, and commences again twenty-seven bars later; the opening of the second group is eliminated in favor of the continual development of the opening theme. This does not suggest an unchallenged reign of a standard form.

In 1774, J.C. Bach was almost forty years old, and he may have been attached to older models. A younger composer, however, exhibited the same variety. Let us take the symphonies Mozart wrote in 1772 when he was sixteen. Several of them, indeed, show the standard recapitulation: K. 124 in G, K. 128 in C, K. 129 in G, K. 130 in F, and K. 132 in E♭, although K. 132 does not repeat either section, and the recapitulation in K. 128 starts with a sequential modulation of the main theme that continues the development. However, K. 120 in D has no development section, and no repeats; in K. 130 in D the recapitulation (bar 100) starts without warning or pause in the middle of the development with bar 14 of the exposition and the opening bars return only at the end; K. 134 in A has repeats but no development section, and the second part begins with a recapitulation of the first group on the subdominant; K. 162 in C has no repeats, and the recapitulation starts with bar 13 of the exposition in the middle of the development; K. 181 in D has no development. It would be hard to persuade me that so a young a composer as Mozart was hanging on to antiquated fashions.

Moreover, the rarity of a form is far less significant than its viability. A recapitulation that begins on IV is rare in the eighteenth century, although it appears from time to time. It persists, however; Schubert liked it and even Beethoven uses it in the Bagatelles op. 126 at the end of his life. It fits with the harmonic sensibility of the period, and remains an option from 1750 to 1830 in spite of its infrequency.

This freedom of choice did not prevent the formation of stereotypes, but the significance of these stereotypes in any given decade from 1750 to 1800 will only be misunderstood by classifying them as deviant forms or by a failure to recognize them as related sonata forms. The history of sonata style cannot be written as a gradual progress toward the nineteenth-century model. Older stereotypes remain viable for long periods. C. P. E. Bach continued to publish until the late 1780s, sometimes using forms of the 1740s—these, indeed, continue to be employed as late as the time of Chopin.

A statistical study of the changing frequency of these stereotypes from 1740 to 1800 is impossible in the present state of knowledge. Too much of the music remains unpublished, the manuscripts often difficult of access: the dates of a very large number of works are uncertain, and the tendency to date forms according to their distance from the canonic nineteenth-century description has turned out to be untrustworthy. In any case, a statistical study would not explain why some stereotypes vanished and others were so durable. Three stereotypes of the 1750s and 1760s that were to disappear must be touched on, as their fragility is instructive for the general history of sonata forms. They weakened with the radical change that marks the beginnings of the Viennese Classical style.

The first of these mid-century stereotypes is a new theme in the dominant minor[4] which appears just as the dominant has been reached in the exposition. This device, which was to become very rare later in the century, enables us to appreciate the strengths and limitations of mid-century style. The dominant minor used for the initial contrasting theme right at the beginning of the second group both strengthens and weakens the tonic-dominant polarity of the exposition. It affirms the movement to the dominant, since the change from V to v emphasizes the dominant as the new fundamental bass tone, but attacks its specific character as a dominant as well as its stability, for the minor mode cannot be used as a dominant—at that time, it was inherently less stable than the major. This stereotype is occasionally found in the Italian opera aria (any out-of-the-way use of the minor mode in the eighteenth century is likely to be laid on the doorstep of the Neapolitan school), but it is essentially a symphonic device, I believe.

It is clear why this stereotype did not last very long: it has only a purely local, small-scale effectiveness. In his earliest period Haydn uses the dominant minor for the first contrasting motif in the exposition after a strong cadence on V: we find it in the principal quick movement of symphonies 1, 2, 4, 5, and 15, all of which (we are told by Robbins Landon) were written by 1761.[5] With symphonies 18, 20, 23 and 27, written a few years later, Haydn adapted this practice to greater efficiency: the minor is no longer the mode of the *initial* contrasting theme of the second group, but occurs somewhat later after the major mode has been fully established and confirmed by a new texture. In this more sophisticated form, the use of the dominant minor in the second group enters permanently into sonata style.[6] The more primitive version—of going directly to the dominant minor to start the second group—appeared somewhat later in Haydn's quartets than in his symphonies, and there is a striking example in his op. 17, no. 6 in D major of 1771, the last such example in the quartets.

The symphonic nature of this stereotype may be verified: Haydn does not use it at all in the string quartets written before opus 9, (either in the original form found in Monn and others, or in his later sophisticated version) and it is rare in his piano trios or sonatas. (One spectacular exception, in obvious imitation of symphonic style, may be found in the silly Sonata in A major, [H.XVI:5], almost certainly not by Haydn.[7]) Haydn's use of the stereotype in the first three string quartets

4. See the Symphonies in D and in G by G. M. Monn, in *DTOe*, vol. 39, and the example quoted above (p. 134) from Scarlatti.
5. Robbins Landon gives no. 15 leeway up to 1763 (misprinted as 1793 on p. 43 of his edition of the symphonies) but prefers to put it back to 1760 for good stylistic reasons.
6. A touch of the minor mode in the passage that leads to the second group (i.e., in the bars just before the half-cadence on V of V) remained standard practice for decades. It does not, of course, attenuate the impact of the dominant when it arrives.
7. See the preface to volume I of Christa Landon's edition of the sonatas, Universal Edition 13337–39.

of op. 9 and in op. 17 no. 6 is in keeping with the evident adaptation of a symphonic breadth and seriousness in these works.

A similar but far more dramatic mid-century stereotype is a recapitulation that opens with the main theme now for the first time in the tonic minor. This again is of Neapolitan origin. Johann Schobert, who worked in Paris in the 1760s, used this effect in his Piano Trio in F major and in the finale of the Piano Quartet in Eb major, op. 7. Mozart also put it into his Piano and Violin Sonata in G major, K. 9, of 1764 where it is followed at once with the major: perhaps the eight-year-old composer should not yet be held responsible, but in any case, Leopold let him write it.[8] This is certainly a trick that loses its effectiveness with repetition. Christian Gottlob Neefe used it in the third of his twelve keyboard sonatas dedicated to C. P. E. Bach and published in 1772, but it largely disappears after 1770, except for one beautiful appearance in Haydn's Symphony no. 47.

Like the use of the tonic minor at the beginning of the second group, the appearance of the tonic minor in the recapitulation became a permanent legacy to sonata style only when postponed for a phrase or two. In later works, the arrival of the tonic minor in recapitulations (frequently as a form of subdominant) is put off until at least a few measures of tonic major have first been sounded. The abandonment of both these stereotypes in their original form comes naturally in the 1770s with the shift away from the mannered dramatic forms of the so-called *Sturm und Drang* period to a more sociable style.[9]

The third stereotype is by far the most important stylistically and statistically: the appearance of the main theme in the tonic with the second phrase of the development. Oliver Strunk, who named this form "premature reprise," observed its great frequency in instrumental music of the mid-century. It can only be considered premature with respect to the model that was to become canonic much later. I quote Strunk's characterization from his fine article "Haydn's Divertimenti for Baryton," an essay still indispensable to all students of eighteenth-century music:[10] "In the divertimenti it occurs in every third or fourth number, beginning with Divertimento 7 (1761 or '62), and often follows immediately on the preliminary restatement of the principal subject in the dominant." We can easily recognize this pattern: it is the traditional beginning of A^2 of the mid-century operatic aria, type 2—probably the most frequently found of the types in the 1750s and 1760s.

8. Wyzewa and Saint-Foix think that Leopold added the turn to the major mode. See Abert, W. A. Mozart, Leipzig, 1956, I, p. 89.

9. The literary movement properly called the *Sturm und Drang* (that small group of undergraduates at Strasbourg University who took Goethe as their chief and Herder as their philosopher) only starts in the early 1770s and so postdates by a few years much of what is called *Sturm und Drang* in music.

10. Published 1932; republished in *Essays on Music in the Western World*, New York, 1974, pp. 126–70.

In his brief discussion, Strunk brings the full weight of his moral disapproval to bear on the "premature reprise."[11] He writes, "In accepting such sterile mannerisms as the 'false' reprise, Haydn defers to the conventions of the time." He also remarks that "Wyzewa and Saint-Foix cite Mozart's early use of this 'more or less comic device' as evidence of his sensitivity to the influence of Haydn and his Viennese contemporaries. Perhaps its employment was more general than has been alleged."[12] (The last sentence is a model of Strunk's reticence or understatement, as this stereotype abounds throughout the music of most of Haydn's contemporaries from 1750 to 1775, as it does in Haydn's own work.)

Clearly, Haydn and his contemporaries did not understand the function of a development section as well as we do today. For the confusion they created, they have only themselves to blame. If, however, one sees the relation of the device of the "premature reprise" to the opera aria, then there is nothing inherently comic about its employment. Pushed slightly later into the development section (but it must be remembered that with many of the works of the 1760s we are often dealing with very short pieces and there would be no room for such manoeuvres), it can indeed be put to very witty use—and is in fact beautifully used in this way by Haydn in the symphonies. The "premature reprise" is a formal convention, a way of beginning the second half of a sonata. Gervasoni, who was as reactionary as the next theorist, still recommends the "premature reprise" as late as 1800 in the *Scuola della Musica:* far from considering it comic, he writes that the two appearances of the theme—at the dominant followed by the tonic—"admirably serve to strengthen the expression and to recall the opening idea of the sonata itself."[13]

In a sense, Strunk was right to call it a "sterile mannerism." His judgment has been ratified by time and history: the convention disappeared, dying gradually in the 1770s. Strunk's prejudice obviously became Haydn's own prejudice and that of his later contemporaries. Why was the device condemned? One answer may be set aside immediately: it was not that composers and public were tired of it. One half of the convention—that of beginning the development with the main theme at the dominant—remained alive and well. In spite of the fact that it was obviously stodgy and old-fashioned and that critics and theorists were complaining by the 1790s (if not before) that it was a dull thing to do, it

---

11. He distinguishes between "premature reprise" (when the first theme never returns again in the tonic) and "false" reprise (when it does)—and then adds "The actual result is very much the same."

12. Strunk, p. 150.

13. ". . . e questi ritorni poi servono mirabilmente a rinforzare l'espressione ed a far risovvenire il primo pensiero della sonate medesima" (p. 467).

continued to be used frequently and with complete satisfaction until well into the twentieth century.

The popularity of "premature reprise" for at least two decades and its subsequent disappearance can be understood in the light of a confused desire for both symmetry and dramatic effect. The need for a balanced symmetry always remained essential to any conception of sonata in all its forms. (Many development sections reveal this, as they take up the complete thematic pattern of the exposition, and develop each theme in turn.) In order to achieve that symmetry, a generation of composers borrowed from the two-part aria form a pattern for beginning the second half of an instrumental piece which was neither two-part nor three-part but something in between. When the movement was short and the style relaxed, no harm was done; but the modern critic, who wishes to be stirred, expects more drama and complains when he does not get it.

A development section properly delays resolution, and resolution is both thematic and harmonic: the essential resolution is that of the second group, which has never been played in the tonic and must be so played before the piece can be considered over, the matter closed. The "premature reprise" followed by a development section gave a symmetrical opening to the second half, and still delayed the resolution of the second group. Only gradually did composers come to believe that avoiding the tonic altogether before thematic resolution would be more effective; only during the 1770s did they firmly equate the final return of the tonic and the return of the main theme—and even then, this more highly articulated return is immediately succeeded by a secondary development section in a large number of cases, almost invariably, in fact, in the most impressive works.

The need for the "premature reprise" can perhaps be better understood together with still another stereotype of the 1750s, one which also appears to irritate modern critics and listeners: the recapitulation that opens only with the *second* phrase of the main theme, and omits the first phrase altogether.[14] This is a common practice in the mid-century symphony. It, too, provides a structure for the second half:

First phrase of main theme	Development	Second phrase of main theme	Second group
V	$\longrightarrow$ vi	I	I

that assures a free symmetrical relation to the first half. (It is probably related to type 3 of the aria, see page 37.) Evidently, composers sometimes had a certain shyness about bringing back the opening bars, par-

14. Haydn's Symphony no. 24 in D major combines this procedure with another of our stereotypes: the reprise begins with the second phrase, now in the minor mode. The symphony dates from 1764.

ticularly when they had already been played a second time at the dominant. This psychological resistance to the modern conception of recapitulation as a simultaneous return to the tonic and the first theme is significant: the second half of the sonata is never really considered as two absolutely separate sections until the nineteenth century.

Before then, too marked a break in continuity, too great a rupture of symmetry must have been distasteful. Even in the 1780s, when the return of the tonic was so generally accompanied by the beginning of the main theme, Haydn can play a wonderful historical joke by recalling an old-fashioned convention. His Quartet in Eb major, op. 50 no. 3 of 1784 begins:

Here is the end of the development with an abortive cadence on vi and the beginning of the recapitulation:

Even the false reprise on IV (bar 82) omits the first four bars of the theme, and so does the return of I at bar 88, a device now out of date for almost twenty years. But Haydn has another trick to play. Here is the end of the recapitulation:

Bar 111 is final, but not quite final enough: the two bars of rest shake one's confidence, however. Perhaps the movement is really over, even if oddly so. Then the missing first phrase returns. This must be one of the rare moments when a knowledge of history is necessary to enhance one's pleasure in Haydn's wit, although the effect is genuinely funny in itself even for those who do not realize that this is a joke on an old-fashioned style.

The "premature reprise" does, I suppose, need some such histori-cal sympathy, or perhaps merely an innocent ignorance of historical prejudice will do. In any case, it is wrong to think of fixed models of so-nata form for the eighteenth-century composer: useful stereotypes that could be employed or abandoned at will are what he probably worked with.

Until well into the nineteenth century, the point of greatest free-dom in a sonata form is the reappearance of the opening theme in the tonic in the second half: where is it placed, how much of the theme must be played, will it be played again later, indeed, is it necessary to play any of it? The great variety of answers to these questions deter-mines the nature and function of the development section and the reca-pitulation. Because of the freedom of the answers, the different forms blend one into the other with little possibility of any systematic clas-sification.

In short, as Strunk observed, the appearance of the opening theme in the tonic at the second phrase of the development did not necessarily imply that the theme would return once again in the tonic or that it would not. If it did not, the form approximated slow-movement form (i.e., without a central development section but possibly with a secon-dary development between the reprise of the first and second groups); if the first theme did return, the form began to approach that of the so-nata rondo. The situation remained fluid until the "premature reprise" disappeared.

This particular stereotype was destroyed by the stylistic revolution of the 1770s. It is then that the functions of the development and reca-pitulation are unmistakably clarified and distinguished as intensifica-tion and resolution respectively. The appearance of the first theme at the tonic early in the development is consequently banished (except when the false reprise is used as a dramatic and very special effect), as it blurs the line between development and recapitulation. In the 1770s the beginning of resolution is usually marked by the return of the opening theme, once again in the tonic (or occasionally the subdominant—Haydn, in the Quartet in D major, op. 20 no. 4, pretends to start the res-olution in IV and wittily switches to I). Thematic and harmonic struc-ture, while still independent, are now more powerfully coordinated.

The new monumentality and the power, even the violence of expression that begins to be apparent in music a few years before 1770 demanded structures whose proportions were clearly defined. The sharpened sense of the function of the different sections of a movement aids in the definition of these proportions, and the management of large key areas made later works of the size of Mozart's *Prague* Symphony possible. The multiplicity of textures within one movement essential to the articulation of the sonata forms was developed from 1730 to 1770, but it was only after 1770 that the transition from one kind of texture to another could be made imperceptibly and with great ease.

The sonata is not yet a specific form even in the 1780s but rather a set of scattered procedures like the mid-century stereotypes, now unified both by the new insistence on large-scale balance of proportions and the awareness of the specific function of long sections and their relation to the movement away from tonic stability and back towards the resolution of dissonance. This new awareness, first visible in the work of Haydn in the late 1760s, was to have its effect eventually on all genres of music, although some of these effects were to be delayed until the coming of Beethoven. Sonata as a form is still a multiplicity; its unity is stylistic, the relation of these many possible procedures to each other in a relatively coherent musical language. By the early 1780s, we may speak of the triumph of sonata style or of Viennese Classicism: all earlier forms, rondo, concerto, fugue, da capo aria, ternary form, have now been turned into sonata forms.

We must not exaggerate the scope of that triumph, in spite of its future prestige. It was European in range, but most evident in the work of Haydn and Mozart. In their operas a large majority of the individual numbers can be elucidated by sonata principles, but this is not true of their contemporary Cimarosa, for example, who rarely makes use of these principles. A sonata exposition and recapitulation—the polarization of material and harmony and its resolution—offered a frame with great flexibility; between them anything was possible, including the introduction of new material, changes of tempi, or nothing at all.

The uncertainty about the function of the development section lasted a long time. One of the piano trios mistakenly attributed to Joseph Haydn but actually by Pleyel, a work in F major, has a development section that begins by rambling on amiably in the tonic for twenty bars. (For those who want to find it, the Hoboken number is XV, 3.) The most astonishing thing about this work is that Haydn sold it as his own,[15] and the misattribution is entirely his fault. This use of the tonic in the development has nothing to do with Beethoven's replaying the main theme at the tonic at the opening of the development of the Piano

---

15. See Alan Tyson, "Haydn and Two Stolen Trios," *Music Review XXII* (1961).

Sonatas op. 31 no. 1 and op. 31 no. 3. There the tonic is only sustained for a few measures—a pulling back into a point of rest before the dramatic modulations that follow. Beethoven's experiment here probably derives from Mozart: e.g., the final of the Quartet in D major, K. 499, where the effect lasts two bars, or from Haydn's late D-major Piano Sonata, H. 51, where the exposition is not repeated, but the development opens as if the repeat were going to be played after all. Mozart also tried the same device—this time only one bar long—in the Piano Trio in Bb major, K. 254.

The essential freedom of the central section of a sonata form explains Haydn's very rare but important use of the sonata with central trio. We have seen this form appear both in the opera and in instrumental works; it can be found not only in the symphonies of Sammartini, but also in J. C. Bach's operas, and in the keyboard sonatas mistakenly attributed to Pergolesi. To the examples already cited from Mozart's operas (see p. 59 above), one must add the Symphony in G major, K. 318, probably also an overture to an opera. Here there is an exposition and full development section before the trio, which is itself in slow-movement sonata form: the recapitulation which follows is in reverse form, holding back the first theme to the end.

Haydn employed this form for special dramatic effect, and it appears even very late in his career. Two important examples are in the symphonies of the 1770s. Symphony in F major, no. 67, has a finale in which a brilliant and effective sonata exposition in alla breve is succeeded by an exquisite *Adagio e cantabile* in ⅜: the recapitulation closes the form, as we would expect. The most beautiful example of this form, however, is the first movement of the *Farewell* Symphony, no. 45, in F# minor.

It is sometimes said that the "Second Theme" of the *Farewell* appears only in the development section, but that makes a "Second Theme" a kind of abstract metaphysical entity which can be incarnated anywhere at all. The "Second Theme" is not merely any contrasting tune, because then we would have second themes in first groups very often indeed, making a hash of the terminology. The "Second Theme" is the new contrasting theme that signals the arrival at the dominant and that confirms the new tonality. There is unquestionably a new theme in the development of the *Farewell*, but its contrast works in a very different way. Here is the entire development followed by the first bars of the recapitulation:

The development opens in the most conventional manner with the main theme at the relative major—properly so, since what is to follow is unconventional although not unprecedented. The new theme appears at bar 108: after thirty-five bars of undeviating *fortissimo* ending with the closing theme of the exposition (bar 102) and a general pause with a fermata, it comes in *piano* and *pianissimo* with a sudden change of key to D major. The horns are silenced throughout, as are the cellos and basses for the first eight bars, and the dynamics never change from *piano* in the entire section. The end is cut off as effectively as the opening: the theme is isolated in the movement, and only the modulation at the very end acknowledges the existence of the rest of the movement —although this section is, in fact, related to what really was a "Second Theme," the new motif that established A major in the exposition:

There is no change of time signature or tempo as in Symphony no. 67: but many trio sections of da capo arias remain in the same tempo and rhythm. The change of key, dynamics, and texture is striking, however, and they are all of a type that characterizes the trio. The central section in D major acts like the trio development section of Sammartini quoted on p. 140, only more dramatically, more operatically—in fact, much closer to the examples Mozart was to write in *Idomeneo* and *Zaide*. This adaptation of an unusual form, one which remained a latent possibility throughout the eighteenth century, is one of Haydn's most brilliant inspirations. Possibly it came from his interest in opera at the time, and the *Farewell* is certainly his most theatrically "staged" symphony.

Perhaps Haydn's most moving and most accomplished example of the sonata with central trio is in one of the last works, the *Creation* Mass of 1801. For a Kyrie, the use of a form with central trio has a large number of precedents: the lowered tension, delicate but expressive contrast, reduced dynamics, and more transparent texture that are so often the attributes of a trio section are very well suited to setting the words "Christe eleison" framed between the two "Kyrie eleison." Mozart's famous unfinished Mass in C minor contains an example. Haydn, in the *Creation* Mass, frames his "Christe eleison" between a sonata exposition and recapitulation. I quote it in full: in so doing, I can kill two birds with one stone, giving not only a late example of an interesting form, but also showing that when the development section is omitted in a work of such dramatic style, the secondary development which begins after the start of the recapitulation takes on extraordinary importance. I leave out the beautiful introduction, although it has important thematic connections with the quick movement that follows, as Robbins Landon had shown;[16] like almost all slow introductions to a sonata form, it turns to the minor mode of the tonic and finishes with a half-cadence on the dominant. Then the Allegro follows:

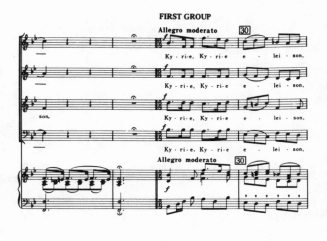

16. See *Haydn*, vol. V, p. 202.

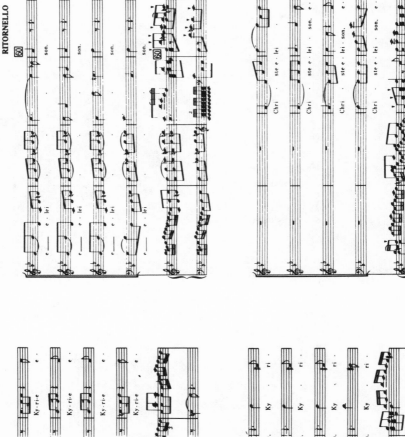

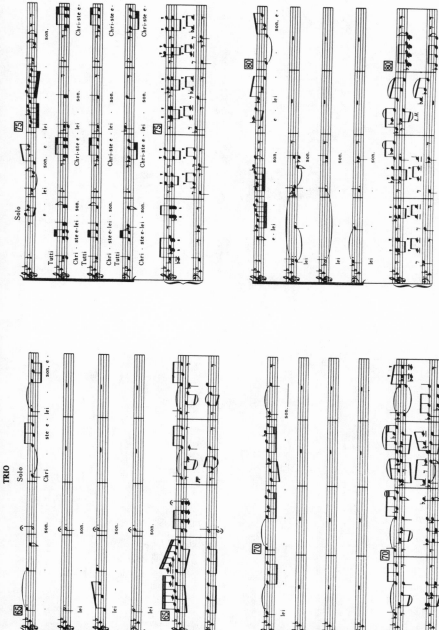

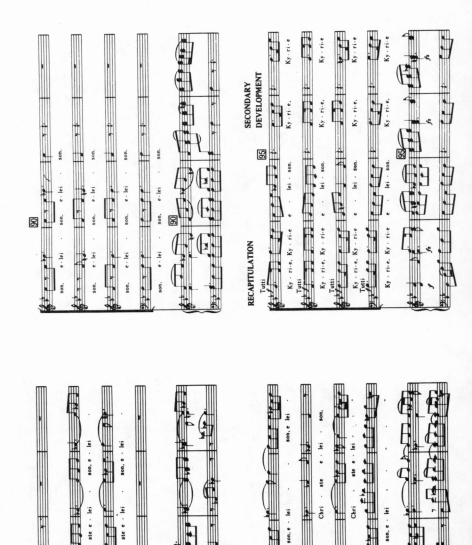

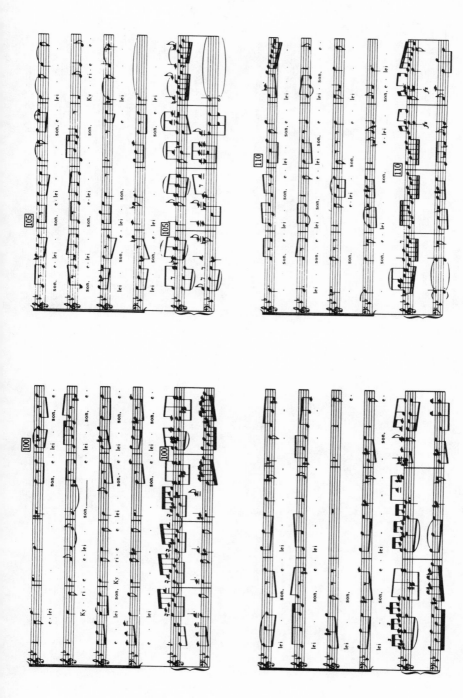

SECOND GROUP

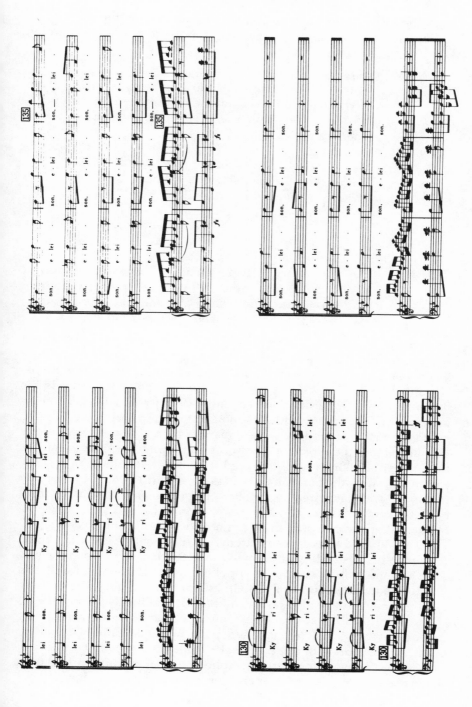

With the elements of concerto technique displayed in the ritornelli to emphasize the general lines of the form, the structure is simple, and in Haydn's monothematic style:

Bars 29–36   First group

    37–46   Ritornello on I and bridge to V (it might appear that the second group would start at 41, but the dominant is not yet emphatic enough, and Haydn works back to a long cadence on V of V in bars 44–46).

    47–60   Second group, variant of main theme with new continuation (bars 47–52), closing theme, bars 52–60.

    60–66   Ritornello on V and short transition

    67–92   Trio. (Binary form.)   a) i→III 67–82
                                               b) III → i 82–92
                                               half-cadence on V.

  93–end   Recapitulation.

    93–95   First group.

  96–119   Secondary development leading to dominant pedal at 107, through IV (111–12) to tonic minor that recalls the introduction and ends on V^7.

  120–end   Recapitulation of second group complete.

This trio (like the one in Sammartini's Symphony in A major) is a short binary form in the tonic minor with an initial cadence in the relative major and a return to the tonic, the most conventional of patterns. Nevertheless, in a work of such large dimensions, Haydn needs the dramatic tension of a development, now displaced until after the reprise of the first theme, which is remarkably short but powerful. The grandeur of this secondary development is such that the half-cadence that introduces the reprise of the second group is much more intense than the similar one that introduced it in the exposition—although a glance will show the parallelism of bars 45–46 and 118–119. The form of the central trio is inspired by the text: this movement is one of the most masterly adaptations of sonata form to a liturgical text and shows the freedom that Haydn could draw upon until the end of his career.

The value of an eccentric pattern like the sonata form with central trio for an understanding of the evolution of sonata style lies in the way it reveals the mobility of the essential aspects of the sonata forms and the different possibilities of realizing them. Tracing this pattern from early Sammartini to early Haydn and Mozart and finally to late Haydn, we can see how the role of a development section becomes increasingly urgent, but that its function is at least partially displaceable. The history of the sonata form with central trio also underlines the impossibility of separating the evolution of the symphony and of chamber music from the contemporary history of opera, concerto, and church music.

VIII ♭   Motif and Function

In his book on the aesthetics of music,[1] written in 1782, Christian Friedrich Daniel Schubart defined the sonata as a "musical conversation, or an imitation of human speech with dead instruments," and wrote an explanation of Italian tempo marks for the German reader. Most of his translations are more or less what one would expect. *Presto,* for example, is "a very fast beat in $^2/_4$, $^3/_8$, $^6/_8$ and other time signatures." Some are defined in terms of sentiment or "affect": *Adagio* is "a slow sad movement." *Allegro,* however, gets a definition very different from the others: "a leading motif, worked out in a somewhat fast movement."

It is significant that the sonata form of the nineteenth and twentieth century was often to be called "sonata-allegro." The motivic structure of the Allegro was evidently plain for everyone to see by 1780, and the new way that the motif was treated in sonata style was essential to the development of the formal structures.

In Haydn, everything comes from the theme, as the composer himself claimed: out of the character of the theme and its possibilities of development arises the shape of the musical discourse. Beethoven carried this a step further: the relation between large-scale structure and theme was equally intimate, but both were worked out together, as recent studies of his sketches have disclosed.[2] He not only made sketches for the themes and for individual passages, but for the work as a whole; the

---

1. *Ideen zu einer Aesthetik der Tonkunst,* written 1782, published 1806.
2. See, above all, the studies by Lewis Lockwood of opus 69 (*The Music Forum,* II, New York, 1970, pp. 1–109) and by Robert Winter of opus 131 (*Beethoven Studies,* vol. II, New York 1977, pp. 106–37).

conception of the entire work took form gradually and influenced the details of the individual themes.

Motivic development has been a basic technique of Western music at least since the fifteenth century, but the use and character of the motif altered radically in the later eighteenth century, evolving with the new conception of musical form. The motif now emphasizes the articulations of form, and—most important of all—is inflected in response to these articulations. One of the first masters of the new technique was Carl Philip Emanuel Bach. Here is the exposition of his Sonata in A major, written in 1765 and published in the *Sechs Clavier Sonaten für Kenner und Liebhaber* (1779).

There are two principal motifs, both announced in the first bar:
A) the staccato parallel sixths (later thirds) of the right hand, here
piano,
B) the little rhythmic figure with repeated notes in the left hand,
forte: ♫ ♫

The two motifs appear at four main points: the main theme where
they establish I; the bridge to initiate the movement to V; the opening
of the second group to confirm the arrival at V; and the closing theme to

round off the exposition. For once the traditional terminology fits a monothematic form like a glove. The relation between large form and motif is:

Bars 1–4:	A and B as first group statement with motif B forte on first two beats, motif A *piano*.
5–8:	Answering phrase *forte:* half-cadence on V (bar 8) marked by shift of B to third and fourth beats.
9–12:	Answering phrase repeated *piano* and arpeggiated.
13–16:	A and B as bridge. Initiation of movement to V: motif A now goes from staccato to legato in one phrase with a more expressive line.
17–26:	Movement to V emphasized by sudden change of texture on V of V, and arpeggiated progression through V of V of V (bar 25), the most important and conventional manner of establishing V as a rival "tonic."
27–30:	A and B as second group to affirm the polarization. The contrast of B and A as *forte* and *piano* respectively is now altered, as well as the contrast *within* a single phrase of staccato to legato. *Forte* and staccato are now opposed together to *piano* and legato, the inner contrast of the phrase replaced by an opposition of two two-bar phrases. The little rhythmic figure, motif B, was previously executed only once in a two-bar group: now the rhythm of its appearance is doubled and it appears once in each bar. The opposition of bars 27–28 with 29–30 pits the dynamic quality of the two motifs against the expressive possibilities that can be drawn from them.
31–38:	Progression to cadence on V. Acceleration of harmonic rhythm (bar 33) in drive to cadence.
39–42:	Motifs A and B appear once more as closing theme. Rhythm of both doubled, A from quarters to eighths, and B appears now twice in each bar. The dynamics of *p* and *pp* emphasize the new lightness.

The motifs are transformed throughout by their function within the form, the second appearance (bar 13) more expressive, the third (bar 27) setting this expressive quality in relief in the most economic way: motif A becomes an isolated sigh in bar 29, a simple appoggiatura that is only resolved in the next bar. The accelerated drive to the cadence elicits the corresponding acceleration of the rhythm of the motifs. In its use of sequence and long stretches of unchanging harmonic rhythm, the movement is still early eighteenth century in style, but the breaks in texture that mark the points of structure are already classical, as is the placing of the articulations.

In this kind of piece, each transformation of the theme demands a different style of playing: the first bars must be in strict tempo with the contrast of dynamics brought out simply: the next two appearances need a more expressive style, above all bars 29 and 30, where the little figure of descending parallel thirds that A has now become must be inflected by a slight *rubato* to bring out its vocal character; the final transformation of the motifs must be played lightly and strictly, the phrasing highly articulated, to bring out its character as a cadential theme.

The structure is elucidated thematically: it is not, in the end, helpful to claim that sonata form is basically harmonic rather than melodic (or even textural/rhythmic). Sonata style is essentially a coherent set of methods of setting the contours of a range of forms into high relief and resolving them symmetrically, and articulation by theme is fundamental to the stylistic language even when, as here, only one theme (essentially the combination of two tiny motifs) is employed. The motifs' brevity makes C. P. E. Bach's technique possible: the changes made for each new point are minimal. Every detail tells.

One essential element of classical motivic technique is not yet present in this sonata. It has the classical hierarchy between principal voice and accompaniment, but no interchange: A is the motif of the principal voice, but it never enters the accompaniment; B is an accompaniment figure, and at no point in the movement does it ever become melody. The final step was taken by Haydn: the motivic accompaniment was already developed by C. P. E. Bach, and Haydn learned how to turn it into melody.

This technique is first worked out by Haydn in the symphonies of the 1770s (although there are earlier precedents for it in his and other composers' works, but less convincingly presented). The incentive to develop this motivic interchange between melody and accompaniment was no doubt the renewed interest in contrapuntal style that appears in Austria in the late 1760s, and finds its finest expression in the early 1770s with the quartets of Florian Gassmann and with Haydn's Quartets op. 20. The revival of the old contrapuntal art with its ideal of equality among all voices of the polyphonic texture (an ideal generally compromised in its realization) was, however, only a halfway house. The real challenge was to retain the late eighteenth-century hierarchy of melodic voice and accompanying parts while giving the accompaniment motivic significance; only then could a true unity of texture be achieved. An accompaniment could occasionally be fashioned out of the motifs of the principal voice, but the most fruitful solution was to learn how to make themes out of formulas of conventional accompaniment. This was Haydn's discovery, and led to some of Beethoven's greatest triumphs.

The simplest way to transform accompaniment into melody—Haydn's favorite device—was to make a theme out of repeated notes. The opening of the Allegro of Symphony, no. 73 in D major of 1781, shows the trick in its most elementary form:

Once the first four notes of the theme have been played in the first violins, everything the second violins play from then on is thematic. Far more astonishing, if more doctrinaire, is the slow movement of the Symphony no. 68 in B♭ major, written around 1778:

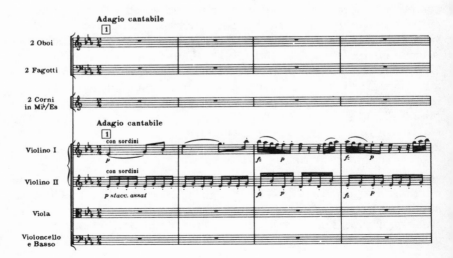

Oboes, bassoons, horns, violas, cellos, and basses suddenly enter *forte* in bar 6, and turn the unobtrusive accompaniment of the muted second violins into fanfare. When the accompaniment continues in bar 7, once again softly in the second violins, but all alone for a full beat, it has become a motif, and at this point we hear it with new ears. This is not an economical way of turning a banal accompaniment into a theme, but it is certainly effective. Haydn seems determined that no one shall miss his innovation. The effect is reproduced three times—accelerated, first after a rest of nine beats, then four beats, then three beats, an extraordinary rhythmic structure. Then immediately in bar 17, the little accompaniment figure becomes the melody transferred to the first violins. Finally, to cap the effect, the banal melodic turn at the end of bars 17 and 19 in the first violins becomes the accompaniment in cellos, basses, and bassoons at bar 25.

Here is the true contrapuntal technique of sonata style: melody and subordinate voices carefully distinguished, yet formed with the same motivic elements. This slow movement is like a sketch, still unrefined, of the famous place in the slow movement of the *Clock* Symphony when the ticking is transferred from the accompanying voices to the solo flute and bassoon. It is significant that during the late 1770s, Haydn experimented in several symphonies with themes made up entirely of accompaniment figures. The second theme of Symphony no. 61 in D major of 1776 is one example:

and the slow movement of Symphony no. 62 in D major of 1780 another. The effect is generally charming if outrageous, as if Haydn were showing off.

The first group of works in which this interchange between main and subsidiary parts is fully exploited throughout is the Quartets op. 33 of 1781. In this set, not only is each instrumental part filled with life (as they already were in opus 20 of some nine years before), but all with the same life, with a unity of motivic development that never sacrifices the clarity and high relief which comes from the distinction between principal line and accompaniment. The moments of ambiguity show this best—those moments when, for a split second, one is not sure where the principal voice is. The beginning of opus 33 no. 1 in B minor has this effect:

In bar 3 the melody is clearly in the cello and the other instruments accompany; in bar 4, one realizes with surprise that the two-note accompanying figure has become the melody, and that the cello is now subsidiary.[3] The trio in the scherzo of op. 33 no. 6 in D major plays the same trick on the listener:

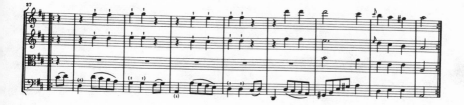

The cello starts with the melody and violins I and II have a little staccato accompanying figure; in bars 31–32, the roles are switched. Without our being able to put our fingers on the exact note when it happens (much depends on the manner of performance), violin I takes the principal part away from the cello. Accompaniment figure becomes melody, melodic figure becomes accompaniment.

I dwell on this point because it seems to me not sufficiently appreciated. Haydn claimed that these quartets were written according to entirely new principles, and although in our time his claim has been called only a commercial slogan, he was fully justified in making it. The new principles are not the motivic development as such—that was indeed old hat even in the quartet writing of 1781—but the unity of the motivic development over all the parts. Larsen is right to emphasize that Haydn's motivic technique was worked out in the symphonies of the 1770s, but the application to the string quartet was entirely new with opus 33. It is above all in the string quartet that we listen most attentively to motivic detail, and where it is most sensitive and most elaborate; symphonic style demanded a larger brush.

3. See a longer analysis of this page in my *Classical Style*, pp. 115–17.

In Haydn, the motif and large structure are intimately bound together: his sonata forms are elucidated by the development of the motif. Since each motif can now penetrate to every part of the work, sonata style becomes a coherent language. In Symphony no. 92 (*Oxford*), the move away from the tonic is made by inflecting a fragment of the opening theme. Here is the counterstatement of the main theme which initiates the modulation to V:

The basic motif is a fragment of the theme, the leap of a tenth in bar 44. The accent and weight of this leap shift through what follows. In bar 44 we have *piano* and  ; bar 45 is *forte*, and the notation changes, indicating more weight ♩ ♩ ♪ . So far the two notes have been equal, and the accent goes normally on the first beat. The movement to instability begins with the next appearance of the leap, bar 47, with the second note longer and heavier than the first, a dotted quarter with a *sforzando*:  ; in bar 49 the first beat is weakened still further by bringing the bass in only on the second beat with a rest on the first beat. In this way the accent of the motif is shifted by a series of graded steps from the stable first beat on to the beat where the accent will cause the greatest rhythmic tension, and the conventional modulation (V of vi to vi, V of V to V) is reinforced by the texture. The *sforzando* of bar 47 dramatizes and makes a surprise out of the move to a B-major triad: the stronger accent in bar 49 emphasizes the greater importance of V of V. The gradations of accent correspond step by step with the harmonic structure.

Haydn's handling of the short motif—two notes are enough—make the fragmentation possible. Beethoven adapted this to an even larger scale. The opening motif of his Symphony no. 8 has its accent initially on the first beat as the phrasing indicates:

At the end of the development section, the accent is shifted to the second beat and repeated stubbornly and insistently over and over:

At the end of the recapitulation, the accent is finally placed on the third beat

so that the accent on the upbeat gives the lift to the rhythm preparing the cadence. The accent of the motif corresponds to its function within each part of the work. This articulation of the changing function of each section sets off the sonata forms from their ancestors; after Haydn and

C. P. E. Bach, the variation of accent in the principal motifs was an important tool in articulating the form.

Beethoven carried the fragmentation even further than Haydn and sometimes reduced a motif to one note. In the Sonata in E♭ major, op. 81a, *Les Adieux*, the motivic basis is a three-note imitation of a soft horn-call:

The sound of the horn became a poetic metaphor for distance, something heard from afar (one finds this effect, for example, in the introduction to Schubert's "Der Lindenbaum"). The end of the introduction inverts the motif:

and the Allegro plays it, adding an expressive written-out appoggiatura to the first note:

which is ![motif], and the *tenuto* on the G and *sforzando* on the E♭ direct the pianist to bring out the motif, made doubly expressive not only by the appoggiatura on its first note, but with the third note, E♭, also made into an appoggiatura dissonant to the harmony and quickly resolved. A motif representing distance now signifies the anxiety and excitement of departure.

The motif is played in minor, simultaneously inverted in the treble and the right way up in the bass as part of the modulation to V:

and is used to conclude the modulation on V⁷ of V:

where the G F Eb at the end is the motif at the original pitch, reharmonized to give it new significance. The same motif is used for the "second theme", which is at the original tempo, as a whole note of the allegro is about equal to a quarter note of the adagio:

and for the closing theme as well:

here played in diminution, eight times as fast. Since the motif consists of three descending notes of the scale, almost all of the intermediate passage-work seems to spring directly from the motif. From the beginning of his career, Beethoven exploited the possibility of using simple sections of scales and arpeggios as themes, and so making the virtuoso passages thematically significant.

The development starts by reducing the three notes of the motif to two:

Then, at last, having made us hear a note simply held for four beats as thematic, Beethoven reduces the motif to one note, repeated many times:

the ultimate fragmentation and the point of extreme tension. This is the end of the development, and the opening of the retransition. The most banal eighteenth-century plan for a development section was to end the development with a cadence on the relative minor, followed by a return to I. This scheme, used many hundreds of times by Haydn and Mozart, was largely abandoned by Beethoven, but he takes it up here. The relative minor is C, and the opening chord of the allegro is an A♭ sixth-chord, with C in the bass. So the old procedure offers Beethoven a return that is surprising, effective, and poetic in its simplicity.

The coda of this opening movement restores the character of the horn call to the motif played with an extraordinary enjambement of tonic entries going softly into the distance:

The bass from bar 243 is a descending scale, and because of its rhythm we accept it as the motif extended. The two descending notes of 252–53 embody one of Beethoven's impossibilities, a crescendo on a sustained note, which the pianist can, in fact, somehow make real—or seem to. The surface of the whole movement is conceived in terms of the transformation of the motif. Everything that takes place in the harmonic structure finds a response in the treatment of the motif in accent and rhythm.

The reduction of a motif to one note is effected elsewhere by Beethoven in a way that determines the large-scale rhythm of a whole sec-

tion. There is a famous shift of accent and periodic rhythm at the end of
the development section of the Fifth Symphony which has caused some
controversy:

The shift can be seen at a glance if one looks at the beginning and the end of the quotation. At the beginning, the phrase starts with an up-beat to an even-numbered bar: 180, 188, 196; at the end with an upbeat to an odd-numbered bar: 229, 241, 249. What happens in between? The theme starts as a four-bar motif with a four-bar answer: 180–187, 188–195. The motif has three long notes (♫♩ ♩ ♩), and the next period reduces them to two notes, with the antiphonal reply of two notes: 196–97, 198–99. The antiphonal movement continues, winds against strings: 200–01 against 202–03; then 204–05 against 206–07. Then the reduction of the motif takes place from two notes to one: 208–09 against 210. The diminuendo from *ff* to *pp* starts precisely with the bar in which the motif appears as one note, 210. The antiphonal exchange, now single bar against single bar, proceeds until the four-bar motif is fully restored at 229, and the eight-bar periodic movement reinstated from 233.

The vehicle of the shift of accent is the ultimate fragmentation of the motif,[4] and the structural point is just before the return of the main theme and the tonic, as it was in the Sonata *Les Adieux*. The large-scale harmonic structure, the texture (here the periodic phrasing, the dy-namics, and the accent of the bar), and the thematic content need to be

---

4. For different considerations on this rhythmic shift, see the article " 'Extra' Measures and Metrical Ambiguity in Beethoven," by Andrew Imbrie in *Beethoven Studies*, I, ed. A. Tyson, New York, 1973, pp. 45–66.

considered together to understand the form[5]—even the instrumentation must be considered, as the effect of this passage depends on the separation of strings and winds and their opposition.

The most radical transformation of a theme is from dissonance to resolution—taking the longest possible view, this is basically what happens in a sonata when the second group is recapitulated at the end in the tonic. This fundamental transformation, however, may be reinforced in detail by changes within the themes. The extreme form of this occurs when a theme remains without a resolving cadence until its last appearance: the famous example is the last page of *Tristan und Isolde* which, for the first time, resolves the opening theme of the Prelude to Act I. In a brilliant essay,[6] Lewis Lockwood has shown that in the first movement of the *Eroica* Symphony, a passage which appears prominently three times leads to a dissonant climax the first two times, and is resolved only at the end of the movement. From a study of the sketches, he demonstrates that this passage was planned almost from the start with this double function, and that it remains constant throughout all the innumerable changes and elaboration imposed by Beethoven both on the musical material and the structure of the movement as he worked on it.[7]

The Sonata in F minor, op. 57, (the *Appassionata*) makes similar use of one of the principal motifs, and the phenomenon is perhaps even more striking because the motif is so short and is used so often. It is the little four-note figure that appears on the first page:

(It is derived from the alternation of F minor and G♭ major of the first eight bars and is a laconic summary, a diminution of that relationship which is fundamental to the work.) This motif brings on the first climax:

5. In fact, because of the orchestration, no one has any difficulty understanding this passage except analysts: the ignorant but attentive listener grasps the extraordinary increase of tension. I am not taking an obscurantist position, merely pointing out that analysis often elucidates with difficulty what we all already understand with ease—which is as it should be.

6. "*Eroica* Perspectives: Strategy and Design in the First Movement" in *Beethoven Studies*, vol. III, ed. A. Tyson, New York, 1980(?).

7. See my *Classical Style* for an analysis of the slow movement of Mozart's Concerto in G major, K. 453, in which the opening theme ends with a half-cadence on V and a fermata

The following chord, which will play an important role in the work, is framed by the motif and traced by the climactic figuration just quoted:

In the bridge to A♭, the motif is augmented, leading to V of III:

and one can find echoes of it in phrases like

but I am largely concerned here with the original form in which the motif remains intact. This original form demands separate treatment, as it articulates the most dramatic events, and is set clearly in relief by Beethoven.

The entrance of this motif invariably marks an explosion. Its second appearance is at the end of the development, and outlines the same chord as that on the opening page:

---

the first four times it appears, and leads directly into a tonic cadence only on its fifth and last appearance after the cadenza.

This is the greatest climax so far, and a stupendous one, unequalled in earlier piano music, I believe. It should lead to the tonic resolution of the recapitulation, but it does not. This refusal to resolve here is the stroke of genius in the work: we can see from the example that the recapitulation opens but the tonic resolution is withheld, the tension prolonged by a pedal on V which turns the harmony into a 6/4 chord. The conception is justly famous.

The 6/4 harmony is continued with extraordinary effect through the entire first page of the recapitulation, including the return of the four-note motif:

The next and final appearance of the motif is in the coda, just before the Più Allegro of the final section. Once again it marks an explosion, the end of a written-out cadenza, *sempre ff*, and once again brings in the original harmony with which it was introduced:

Here, the pedal insistently sustains the harmony, with its clash of C/Db. The resolution comes at last with bars 239–40 and the Più Allegro. This is the first time that the motif is resolved, and, with a decisive V-I cadence, it opens the final section which remains in the tonic throughout. This is the first time, too, that the motif—even in its transformed and more allusive forms—leads to anything except a dominant of whatever tonality controls the passage. The motif, in short, articulates every important climax and, with extraordinary brevity and concentration, the final resolution. It is a monad of the universe in which it exists, serving as a tiny mirror: its tension and resolution are those of the entire structure.

In the sonata forms, the meaning of a phrase depended on its place in the work as a whole, on its position in the general movement from polarization to resolution. The forms, therefore, demanded clearly separable elements whose altered functions could be clearly recognized as they appeared at different points of the work. These isolated elements, idiosyncratic and individual, are also permutable: the order of their appearance can be changed. The danger of the sonata forms is, indeed, that the thematic elements, some of them highly characteristic, are so easily separated and rearranged that the work loses its continuity and falls to pieces in the hands of the incompetent composer. These elements, however, defined with extraordinary clarity, stand out from one another in high relief.

The *Prague* Symphony, Mozart's most massive achievement in the symphonic genre—a work which unites grandeur and lyricism as no other—shows this play of individual and permutable motivic elements at its highest. (See pp. 202ff.) The motivic structure of the main theme is so complex, indeed, that Mozart did some exceptional sketches for the opening of the Allegro. The multiplicity of motifs in the statement is astonishing. The opening phrase reveals the same relation between main voice and accompanying voices and the same ambiguities that we have observed in Haydn's symphonies and quartets, accomplished with a delicacy, even a smoothness of surface that was not in Haydn's range. The ambiguity commences in the first bar (bar 37): is the syncopated violin line melody or accompaniment? Bar 38 continues the doubt, which is resolved with bar 39—the first violin line is accompaniment, the melody lies in the lower instruments. Or does it? In bar 41, in which very little is changed and all the voices continue uninterruptedly their individual lines, the balance has tipped the other way: violin I is now principal voice, the others accompany. This is the ultimate form of the classical principle of the obbligato accompaniment discussed above (pp. 174 ff) where accompanying voice may be transformed into principal voice and vice versa. (*Text continues on p. 221.*)

STATEMENT

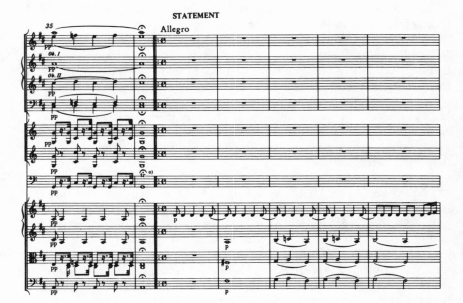

COUNTERSTATEMENT

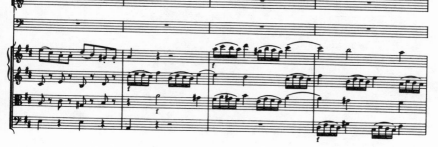

PRINCIPAL THEME

*) Zu T. 133 in den Flöten und Oboen vgl. Vorwort und Krit. Bericht.

*) Zu T. 142 in den Trompeten vgl. Vorwort und Krit. Bericht.

"RECAPITULATION " OF A

RETRANSITION
PRINCIPAL THEME ON V, IN THE TONIC MINOR

SECONDARY DEVELOPMENT

etc.

Violin I introduces two motifs:
1) The syncopation: ♪♩ ♩ ♩ ♪♩♪
2)

Violin II produces a third motif with the important C♮:
3)

The brass and winds bring in two more motifs in bar 43, played together contrapuntally. The motif in the flutes and oboes does not reappear again until the development, where it provides the main material.

The counterstatement (bars 45–50) introduces a new counterpoint to the main theme. At each playing of the main theme, there is an alteration—sometimes slight—which elucidates its new significance. The added counterpoint in the oboe emphasizes the C♮, the most important dissonance of the statement, and underlines the harmonic instability of the theme. The tonic is further defined by a new motif in Violin I played against motif 2 in the lower strings (bars 51–54). Then the full orchestra presents three different motivic sections, relatively conventional, but worked out with an elaborate and exhilarating brilliance. The three sections, while largely of the same character, are highly individual: they are labelled *A, B,* and *C* in the score.

> *A:* bars 55–62
> *B:* bars 63–65
> *C:* bars 66–71

The repeated note at the end of *C* leads directly back to the syncopations (motif 1) of the main theme. This third section begins the modulation with the emphatic half-cadence on V, an overemphatic half-cadence in reality, as its force implies a dynamic movement away from the tonality that has so far been established.

Mozart now turns to a procedure that is much more typical of Haydn: he recalls the main theme in order to move to the dominant. At this point in an exposition, Mozart is generally already in V — or else, when he is working on a large scale—and the *Prague* is the largest he was ever to attempt—he introduces a new theme. Here, however, the recall of the main theme has two advantages: its breadth, which is complex and restless; and, above all, the ostinato on the tonic in the first violins. Transposed up a fifth, the ostinato is now on the dominant. The theme, transposed, is *on,* but not yet *in,* the dominant: the subtlety of the procedure is that coming after a half-cadence on V, but still *in* I, the theme picks up the repeated A of the previous phrase and effects the modulation to V as it goes along, simply by being played.

One alteration of the theme is made: the E in the second violins (the initial note of motif 3) is sharpened throughout, increasing the restlessness of the theme, and pushing it toward the dominant, A major (bars 71–77). What follows is a return to the four bars that came immediately after the counterstatement (bars 51–54), transposed now to the dominant, and turned into an extensive development (bars 77–95). The texture we call "development" has its proper place here and is almost invariable in Haydn's work; we are less certain to find it in Mozart. The contrapuntal style, the sequential movement, the fragmentation of the themes—all of this signifies that the function of this passage is not the exposition of a theme but harmonic movement: in this case, the affirmation of the dominant, giving it sufficient force and solidity to follow the unprecedented breadth and majesty of the first group in the tonic. This rising bass of the last seven bars drives with increasing excitement towards a full cadence on V, a cadence which is delayed by vi.

The purpose of the delay becomes apparent at once: the second theme begins three notes before the cadence is actually accomplished, and it opens and continues with the simple formula used for the cadence. The break in texture is both clearly set in relief and overridden by the entrance of the new theme: in fact, we do not even know that the theme has started until it is well into the next bar. Thematic and harmonic structure are, therefore, very slightly out of phase, a sophisticated technique that achieves the continuity that the eighteenth-century theorist (like Koch) thought necessary for the symphony, in contrast to the solo sonata.

This theme, too (bars 94–121), is given a breadth commensurate with the whole movement. The theme is in ternary form: major (minor) major. This is a pattern for a second group that became influential, and was often adopted by Schubert and Dussek. The turn towards the minor in the second group was, by the end of 1786, when the *Prague* was written, a stereotype of classical sonata style (see above, p. 154). (Note that the entrance into the return of the major mode, bar 111, has an overlapping similar to the opening of the theme, and with an even lovelier grace.)

This theme is rounded off like the first theme by the three brilliant motifs *A*, *B*, and *C*. Larsen has called attention to the ritornello character of this procedure, derived from the concerto.[8] What is most original here, however, is the permutation of the elements. The two ritornello sections are, in fact, very different. The structure of the closing section is

> *A:* bars 121–24
> *C:* bars 125–27
> First theme in inverted counterpoint: bars 129–35
> *B:* bars 136–140

This is because *B* is the most brilliant and stable of the three, and *C* leads—as before—directly into the main theme with its repeated notes. These (motif 1) are powerfully stated by trumpets, horns, cellos, basses,

---

8. *The Mozart Companion*, ed. Robbins Landon and Mitchell, New York, 1969, p. 189.

and tympani (bar 129). The main theme has by now been employed to open the tonic section, to initiate the modulation to V, and to close the section in V as well: each appearance has demanded a change, the last being the most considerable, with the theme played *forte* for the first time.

The development is based above all on the theme given to flutes and oboes at the opening of the allegro (bars 43–44), motif 2 of the main theme, and ritornello motif *A*. This is Mozart's contrapuntal art at its greatest, very much kin (even thematically) to the fugue in the overture to *The Magic Flute*. The development is a traditional one, however, in two respects: the opening phrase at the dominant is immediately replayed in the tonic, a version of the "premature reprise" which passes almost unnoticed as it only uses part of the main theme, and the vigor of the contrapuntal texture carries the movement onward without a break (bars 143–54).

There is a clear distinction in the *Prague* between the development proper and the retransition. This distinction is made neither by a cadence nor by a break in the texture: like thousands of other examples in the eighteenth century, the development proper moves towards a cadence on the relative minor vi (here B minor), but the cadence never comes; what enters instead is the ritornello section *A, B,* and *C* complete with tonic. Since *A* has been as important element of the development, this is accomplished with great ease. The tonic enters naturally as part of a sequence (bars 176–80), and a good part of the first group is played before the entrance of the main theme in the tonic but *on* the dominant. After the end of the development proper, the retransition brings the main theme again, with an alteration, slight but wonderful, to make it fit its new function (bars 189–208). This time the function of the theme is to prepare its own return: accordingly it does what almost all introductions did at that time, turns to the tonic minor on a dominant pedal in order to bring back the major. The F♯ of the theme is changed to an F♮; the counterpoint in the winds is their original completion of the main theme, now combined with it.

The recapitulation begins, therefore, after some of its work has already been done: motifs *A, B,* and *C* have been replayed in their original order in the tonic, and the main theme, used previously at (but not *in*) the dominant to establish V, has returned in the same way to reestablish I. Mozart prepares the recapitulation by recapitulating, announces the tonic with the tonic. I do not wish to give the impression that this is an exceptional procedure; Mozart is using a technique here developed and employed many times over by Haydn and other composers. It is perfectly reasonable to achieve the retransition by using part of the first group in the tonic to precede the reentry of the opening theme. (Less usual is the employment of part of the second group now in the tonic for the retransition, but that, too, is found.)

The recapitulation[9] omits the ritornello section already played in the tonic in the development; the counterstatement leads to an exceptionally lovely Secondary Development which goes from bars 219 to 227. It does not replace the "bridge" in order to keep the material in the tonic. Oddly enough, at the end (bar 228) it even seems to go to the dominant, and Mozart is then obliged to rewrite the "bridge" in order to move back to I. The Secondary Development exists for its own sake, or, rather, for the sake of its magical progression which serves to counteract the tonic-dominant polarity. It introduces the subdominant area (the subdominant minor and then the even more remote flatted submediant). It cannot be emphasized too much how traditional is this move to the subdominant directly after the beginning of the reprise: from the opera aria to the solo sonata, it is an important element of classical harmonic structure, so important that not even the eighteenth-century theorists overlooked it. It has been omitted from the standard definitions of sonata form because the nineteenth century lost the feeling for the opposition of dominant against subdominant.

It is rare, of course, for the Secondary Development and the move to the subdominant to be given such depth of feeling and such poignance as they are here by Mozart. It is his last alteration of that extraordinary main theme, except for some remarkable chromatic harmony added to its final appearance in the ritornello section at the end. The rest of the recapitulation is fairly straightforward, like the recapitulation of the *Eroica* once the Secondary Development is over; a structure so massive needs a considerable amount of absolute symmetry for the resolution to be convincing. The *Eroica* needs a long coda as well to counterbalance the enormous development: Mozart contents himself with playing the main theme twice within the final ritornello orchestrated for full brilliance, the second time with the two principal voices reinverted to their original position. Once again, in this work, we can see the reciprocal relation between motif and structure in a sonata form: the motif articulates structure, emphasizes the most crucial points, and the structure reinterprets the motif, giving each appearance a new and sometimes radically different significance.

The Symphony in D major, no. 31, of 1765 by Haydn (called the *Hornsignal*) teaches a brilliant lesson in articulating a form by instrumentation. The structure is wittily defined by the solo instruments: the principal solos are the flute and the horns, which imitate a posthorn—an instrument that can only play the notes of the triad (here D, F♯, A). Each has a motif. The flute has a scale:

---

9. Larsen (*Mozart Companion*) writes that only the second part of the exposition is recapitulated, but this is misleading.

and the post-horn has a signal:

The movement opens with a fanfare for the horns followed by the signal motif:

The signal is played at the following points in the movement:

Exposition: 1) Second phrase of first group.
                  Signal on D.
                  2) Final phrase of exposition. Closing theme and
                  confirmation of V.
                  Signal on A.

Development: 1) End of development proper, just before cadence
                  on relative minor, vi (B minor).
                  Signal on F♯.

Recapitulation.   Note: After the end of the retransition with a half-
                  cadence on V and a two beat pause, there is a
                  surprise. The opening phrase (fanfare for horns)
                  does not return. Instead the closing theme *in the
                  minor* is played softly (marked *piano* and without
                  the double basses; bar 111). Then the major mode
                  returns with the second phrase (bar 119):

1) Second phrase: Return of major mode.
   Signal on D.
2) Penultimate phrase with closing theme.
   Signal on D.

The last bars of the movement give us the return of the opening fanfare, omitted at the beginning of the recapitulation.

The solo flute fills the gaps, by marking the important moments where the solo horn does not play its motif. These are:

Exposition: Arrival at the dominant in the center of the exposition.

Development: Sequence from IV to V and then to vi. The latter is emphasized by the horn. Flute plays its scale at IV and V.

Recapitulation: Parallel to the exposition.

When the flute plays its scale, the rest of the orchestra is silent, so its motif is in high relief. The hornsignal is accompanied softly.

The first phrase of the reprise, with its surprising minor mode and closing theme, allows the hornsignal both to start the major mode and emphasize the beginning of the reprise of the tonic, and still enter only with the second phrase, just as it did in the exposition. The reprise of the sonata forms demands both a reinterpretation of the exposition and a free symmetry.

The structural events outlined by motif and orchestration are the traditional ones: 1) establishment of I; 2) arrival at V; 3) confirmation of V; 4) sequential movement of development; 5) cadence on vi ending development proper; 6) reappearance of I; 7) final cadence. It must have amused Haydn to make most of his points by imitating an instrument that could only play three notes. Withholding the tonic major at the beginning of the reprise produces a moment of exquisite charm, and the effect is as witty as anything in Haydn. The divisions of the form are clarified in an eccentric way, and their functions beautifully defined; the eccentricity ends by identifying the stylistic norm.

IX   Exposition

THE EXPOSITION OF A sonata form presents the thematic material and articulates the movement from tonic to dominant in various ways so that it takes on the character of a polarization or opposition. The essential character of this opposition may be defined as a large-scale dissonance: the material played outside the tonic (i.e., in the second group) is dissonant with respect to the center of stability, or tonic. Sonata style did not invent this concept of *dissonant section*, but it was the first style to make it the generating force of an entire movement. This opposition may be achieved by a variety of procedures. I enumerate some of the simpler, and some of the subtler ones, and summarize part of the previous discussion.

1) The simplest procedure is a half-cadence on the dominant of the dominant, with a clear break in texture. For this to work properly, the half-cadence on V of V must be preceded by some reference to V of V of V:

From this 1783 Piano Sonata in B♭ Major, K. 333, of Mozart, I have given the counterstatement of the first theme, in which the modulation is gracefully accomplished. V of V of V (the G-major triad) is a continually suggested presence, as the B naturals begin to appear in bar 15, after the first move from V of V to V, which clearly needs reinforcing before we accept the tonicization of V. The method used by Mozart is popular, but I do not know if it occurs more often than some others. It appears to be normal here largely because it is so well done.

A half-cadence on V followed by a new theme on the dominant is frequently seen. This can be repeated in the recapitulation and followed by the new theme at the tonic. In its simple form Haydn obviously found this beneath him, but Mozart evidently liked the naivete of the procedure.[1] It can be used without any sophistication, but the more interesting examples show Mozart sensitively rewriting the bars before the pause in the recapitulation so that the pause on V will point back to the tonic, and not away from it. This is done by referring to the subdominant just before the half-cadence. We have an example of this early in Mozart's career with the symphony in G, K. 129, written when he was sixteen. Here are the two parallel passages:

---

1. Robert Winter has a forthcoming paper on this important stereotype, which he calls the "bifocal close."

RECAPITULATION

2) Another very common procedure that remained useful from the middle of the eighteenth century until late in the nineteenth is a sudden move to the dominant of the relative minor, and the following sequence:

V of vi to vi;
V of V to V;
V of V of V to V of V;
V.

There are thousands of examples of this, but I have already given one by Haydn from the *Oxford* Symphony on p. 188. This is more dramatic than the previous method. A similar sequence often found is

V of ii to ii;
V to I;
V of V to V.

Leaps to still more distant harmonies or to the tonic minor are frequent; they serve to dramatize the movement to V. Most dramatic is an ellipse, like Beethoven's in the Piano Sonata in F major, op. 10 no. 2 (1796–98), where a procedure starting with V of iii is initiated, and then all the intermediate steps are skipped:

In this case, part of the work of establishing the new key must be done by the new theme itself.

3) Merely going to the dominant and staying there will not work (with the minor mode, the move to the relative major is less problematic). What follows must still return to V of V and almost always to V of V of V as well—at least if the music has any ambition. In Dussek's Piano Sonata in A major, op. 43 (written before 1800), the simple move to V seems to require a gigantic half-cadence later on V of V. I give the end of the first theme, and the bridge with the first two bars of the second group:

This is an absurdly lavish, if splendid, way of arriving at V of V. (It is clear that one has arrived at the dominant early on in this passage, and even clearer that Dussek wants his pause on V of V anyway.) The movement also provides a late but idiosyncratic example of "premature reprise." Towards the beginning of the development section, the end of the first theme (with which our quotation began) returns at the tonic, after which the passage quoted is repeated as a development (Dussek is equally prodigal with notes to reach V of vi); then the second group enters in the tonic. There is an elaborate Secondary Development, going to the tonic minor and to the flatted submediant before reaching the subdominant.

4) Changes of texture and rhythm occur at the point of departure from the tonic, at the arrival at the dominant, and at the confirming cadence. There are always two very significant breaks in the harmonic rhythm—and very often a pause as well—to mark the two events of the exposition: just before the beginning of the second group and at the end of the entire section.

The sectional division of the exposition allows a number of possibilities. Two strongly contrasted sections are frequent, the first establishing the tonic center and then moving away; the second containing the dominant group and a final cadence. The first section always has an increasingly animated texture; this is as essential to the style as the modulation itself, and, indeed, helps to give the modulation its dramatic meaning. The dominant section—while it may frequently have a rhythmic animation toward the end that is demanded by a burst of solo or orchestral virtuosity and that also, generally speaking, conserves the Baroque drive toward the cadence—has a harmonic rhythm that opposes this increasing animation starting with a more rapidly moving harmonic rhythm and ending in a much more stable one.

5) Other schemes are possible, notably a binary division of the exposition in which the *second* section, not the first, initiates the modulation as well as confirms it. Examples are Mozart's G-minor Quintet, K. 516, and Haydn's Quartet in B♭ major, op. 50 no. 1. The first section in this scheme has a strong cadence on the tonic. It is sometimes said that in the G-minor Quintet of Mozart the second theme is in the tonic. It would be less misleading to say that the modulation is achieved within a second theme, which takes a new and more expressive form once the new tonality has been established. A second theme (or even a third, fourth, fifth, sixth, and seventh theme) may occur anywhere in a sonata exposition. *The* Second Theme is a metaphysical reification that we could do without.

6) The alternation of regular (periodic) and irregular phrasing or changes of period are essential in defining the texture, and in making the articulations of the structure. There is place here to note only one basic pattern which appears frequently in expositions and which reinforces the sense of increasing animation. A periodicity is set up, then halved, but the smaller units are added together and imply a single period longer than the first. I give two examples from the thousands possible, the first from Beethoven's Sonata, op. 2 no. 1, the second from the Mozart Symphony in E♭, K. 543:

The phrase-lengths (in numbers of bars) are 2, 2 and 4, but if the last phrase is twice as long as the others, it is made up of smaller units. The right hand of bars 5–8 divides (by analogy with the first phrases) as 1 + 1 + 2, and the last two bars, in fact, are divided further by the left-hand pattern (which makes 1/2 + 1/2 + 1/2 + a rest). The longer unit, therefore, imposes an acceleration; here, it leads naturally to a fermata or complete break in texture, and sets off the statement of the theme.

The pattern is similar here in the Mozart Symphony: 4 bars + 4 bars + 6 bars. Once again the longer six-bar phrase divides into 2 + 2 + 2. This inner acceleration leading to a larger continuity—an increased animation integrated within a larger and slower movement—is an essential device for sonata style in handling the complexity of texture, and one may observe its effect in the technique of development.

7) It may be useful to summarize articulation by theme briefly here. A new theme of distinctly different character may arrive when the modulation to the dominant has been completed. This new material, named, since the nineteenth century, second theme or opening of the second group was called the "characteristic passage" (by Galeazzi) in the late eighteenth century. An opposition of themes at this point is employed by the Mannheim symphonists but rarely by Philip Emanuel Bach; it is also more typical of Mozart than of Haydn.

To articulate the movement to the dominant, instead of a new theme, the first theme may be played in the new key; or a variant of the theme—generally more complex, more swiftly moving, and unstable— may be played. This method, favored by Haydn, requires a longer and more varied modulatory section between the opening and the section in the dominant. In fact, when the principal theme is used at the opening of both tonic and dominant sections, the modulation is itself generally initiated by an important thematic change.

Even when the themes are not transformed, the sharp distinction between the functions of the various formal sections that is the essence of the sonata forms gives each appearance of a theme a different significance. The main theme of one of Haydn's "monothematic" forms takes on a radically different meaning when it reappears in the exposition at the dominant to initiate what is called the "Second Group." This is largely because of the way it is prepared and introduced. In the concerto grosso of the early eighteenth century (from which Haydn's technique may be derived), the second ritornello may bring the main theme back on V, after a solo section has been closed and rounded off with a full cadence on V. In Haydn's monothematic form, however, the return of the main theme on V either brutally interrupts a previous passage in the tonic (in which case the main theme initiates the modulation) or it is prepared by a half-cadence on V of V. In either case, the previous section is not fully rounded off, and the theme appears to interrupt or to complete a cadence. Whatever the origins of the reappearance of a main theme at V, this new sense of articulation transforms the device. (The reappearance of the main theme at the *end* of an exposition, however, retains much of its kinship with the concerto.)

The confirming final cadence is always set in relief thematically. If there is a new theme at the opening of the second group, then the opening theme or a variant may return as a cadence, framing the exposition. If the first theme is used again at the opening of the second group, then the cadence is almost always marked by a new theme (closing theme).

Although the distinction between the two opposing levels, tonic and dominant, may be marked by the number and variety of themes, the stability of the tonic is often emphasized by two successive performances of the opening theme: statement and counterstatement. The statement must therefore end with a full cadence on I, or half-cadence on V. The dominant group, always in some sense more animated, is contrasted with the tonic, particularly by Mozart, by a larger succession and greater variety of themes of an expressive character. The final cadence is almost always marked, even when there is a new closing theme, by a series of conventional flourishes, which repeat and embellish a V-I cadence.

At the end of the exposition, in order to confirm the new harmonic center, a considerable amount of insistence upon the now-tonicized dominant is called for. At this point, the most conventional material is often found, with cadential phrases repeated many times over. As eighteenth-century theorists remarked, the section in the dominant is longer that that in the tonic.

In sum, the number and variety of themes are not determinants of form, but even when only one theme is used, it must serve to articulate the polarization. In monothematic works there are, therefore, always a significant number of subsidiary motifs or even conventional passages, which may not arrive at a sufficient level of individualization to be considered themes, but which serve to set the structure in relief.

In most accounts of sonata form a great deal is made of the principle of contrasting themes. It seems to me that once the idea of articulating a form by using a new theme to set off the arrival at the dominant comes into being, it is inevitable that the majority of the "second" themes will have a character that contrasts sharply with the "first." Anything else would demand a perverse and fanatical attachment to the old-fashioned doctrine of the unity of the sentiment—and this unity, as the North Germans continued to maintain for much of the latter part of the eighteenth century, was best achieved by a form that was monothematic. There is, after all, no point in having two themes if they do not provide some kind of contrast. I suppose one could make a case for claiming that the South Germans and the Italians liked variety for its own sake more than the rest of Europe, but I should hate to have to marshal evidence for that; there is a lot of room for variety of effect in unity of sentiment as Philip Emanuel Bach practiced it. The opposing demands of unity and variety of theme were reconciled by Haydn and, above all, by Beethoven, who used radically contrasting themes clearly derived from the same basic material.

South German and Italian styles did tend to be lighter than the grim manner more popular in the north, so they naturally made room for more tunes, but this has little influence on the historical development of sonata forms, as the monothematic pattern transforms its single theme radically to correspond to demands of the style. Some of the transformations are so thorough as to appear like new themes; this inevitably approximates Haydn's and Beethoven's practice.

Contrast of character is dependent on contrast of function. The opening theme defines the key; that is why most opening themes make heavy use of the three notes of the tonic triad. This insistence on an immediate and unmistakable definition of the tonality by the theme is typical of the style of the last quarter of the eighteenth century; that is why the themes of the lesser composers of this period (and often of the greatest) are, in themselves, less expressive and less characteristic than those of earlier decades. No fully mature sonata form could be initiated by the themes of most of Bach's fugues, or even of most of Scarlatti's sonatas. The opening themes of the classical period are often more neutral, more obviously and explicitly dependent on the tonic triad than those of the Baroque. This is also why thematic resemblances are not in general very impressive in themselves. There may be a lot of permutations of the twelve notes of the chromatic scale, but not so many of the three notes of the tonic triad. The underlying structures of a great many opening themes of the classical period are inevitably bound to be almost identical. Resemblances of rhythm and of texture are consequently far more persuasive than those of pitch in thematic relationships.

The first theme not only defines the tonic but proclaims the importance of the work. If a composer wished (as Haydn often did) to base a large movement on a relatively unpretentious theme or on one which does not begin by outlining the tonic triad, then he generally wrote a slow introduction to precede the allegro. Introductions give importance to quiet openings, define the tonic, and almost invariably move through a turn to the minor mode into a dominant pedal and a half-cadence on V. They are best viewed rhythmically as large-scale upbeats, and harmonically the dominant pedal is the most important element in their structure—and in their emotional effect as well, as it creates a sense of something about to happen. Once slow introductions became more common in symphonies around 1780, it was perhaps inevitable that they would be more closely integrated with the allegros that followed, not only thematically but also by their reappearance later in the faster tempo. One finds this even in the operatic aria: both Haydn's *Armida* of 1783 and Florian Gassmann's *La Contessina* of 1770 have examples in which part of the slow initial section appears later, renotated in the new rhythm. Haydn's *Drumroll* Symphony (no. 103) and Beethoven's Trio for Piano and Strings in E♭, op. 70 no. 2, are the most famous examples of this technique. Reappearances of the introduction in the original tempo later in the movement are also to be found: the *Drumroll* Symphony offers an example of this as well, as do Mozart's Viola Quintet in D major, K. 593, and Beethoven's *Pathétique* Sonata, op. 13.

"Second" themes have their tonalities already defined for them by the previous modulation, and the importance of the work has been established by then—if not, it would be hopeless to do anything about it. They enjoy the luxury, consequently, of displaying more expressive qualities, of being "characteristic," as the eighteenth and early nineteenth centuries termed it. Since they do not define but merely confirm a key, their harmonic rhythm is generally slightly faster than that of the main theme, the reliance on a tonic triad often less emphatic.

8) Modulation in an exposition demands preparation; it is here that we find one of the most revolutionary aspects of sonata style. For a true polarization to take place, the movement to the dominant cannot be the sequential movement dear to the early eighteenth century but requires drastic measures—more drastic in a work of any size than a brief hint of V of V of V, followed by a half-cadence on V of V. The establishment of V as a new tonic opposed to the first constitutes a relation of dissonance, which therefore needs affirmation within the work. The dominant is conceived as a *dissonant tonality* in the exposition.

The two principal sources of musical energy are dissonance and sequence. On a large scale dissonance is by far the more powerful. To keep a piece going, the *early* eighteenth century relied chiefly on sequence—a harmonic movement with the propulsive force of rhythmic repetition. The extension of dissonance to the level of the large structure, however, is largely the invention of sonata style and it is the dramatic tension of the prolongation of this dissonance with its balancing resolution that is the quality common to all the various sonata forms.

The polarization, in fact, leads to the concept of a *dissonant section*, which raises the dissonant interval or chord to a higher power: that is, a simple reintroduction of the tonic key will no longer serve as a resolution, but the section outside the tonic needs to be resolved as a whole. The exposition is therefore conceived in terms of its eventual recapitulation in fully developed sonata style, and the modulation is a dynamic movement that establishes the dissonance of what follows.

The dissonant harmonic values implicit in the thematic material have no longer a simply expressive purpose, but serve to prepare the modulation. Haydn was the first composer to relate the dissonances in the opening thematic material coherently to the large structure; Philip Emanuel Bach, from whom he learned so much, was even more sensitive to the expressive properties of dissonance, but less consistent in his structural use of it, With Haydn, therefore, all of the new elements—in phrasing, rhythm, harmony, and accompaniment figures—and the new sense of form are finally drawn together in sonata style. In Mozart's works, the modulation will often spring from the introduction of new material or from the introduction of unexpected dissonance into the counterstatement of the opening theme. Haydn, on the other hand, often repeatedly emphasized a dissonant element in the main theme until it produced the modulation for him. These two schemes evidently demand different kinds of thematic material and result in different arrangements of texture.

The polarization establishes a movement clearly to the "sharp" side, or dominant. In the various eighteenth-century sonata forms, the subdominant could not be used in the exposition except in the most cursory way. (The practice after 1800 will be briefly discussed later.) It is true that in 1796 Galeazzi speaks of the rare possibility of going to the subdominant in an exposition (which he calls simply "the first part"), but if he knew of an example he failed to mention it.[2] Other writers refer only to the dominant (and the relative major for pieces in the minor). One or two anomalies occur, the strangest being Boccherini's Quintet, op. 25 no. 6 of 1778, where there is a sonata exposition with a first theme in A minor, a second in C major, and third and fourth themes in A major! It is perhaps best to classify this work as a singularly lax misunderstanding of the stylistic possibilities.

9) The interchange between harmony and rhythm may be demonstrated by an oddity of some classical expositions: a move away from the tonic may be felt as imperative if the initial cadence of the statement on the tonic has been too emphatic, too final. It is very difficult to do this well; Mozart was a master of it, and the Piano Sonata in F major, K. 332, of 1778 is a beautiful example:

2. We may find some examples much earlier in the century from Vivaldi and C. P. E. Bach. A pupil of the latter, Johann Gottfried Müthel, wrote an exposition that goes to IV in the first movement of his Sonata in G major for Harpsichord, published in 1756 (modern edition edited by L. Hoffmann-Erbrecht).

Not only are the cadences too emphatic, there are too many of them. The first theme has an inner cadence on the tonic (bars 8–9), and finishes conclusively there (bar 12). The fanfare that follows stays close to the tonic throughout: it has no less than three cadences on I (bars 20, 21, and 22). A quick move to another key is inevitable.

10) The second theme of this sonata (K. 332) has a ternary form that was later to be adopted by Schubert and many others:

A (bars 41–56): lyrical theme in major mode.
B (bars 56–70): developmental texture (fragmentation and sequence) in minor.
A (bars 71–81): lyrical theme (related to bars 41–56) in major.
Closing themes (bars 82–93).

Ternary groupings for first themes are more rare, but they are found in Schubert (see below p. 258).

11) The three-key exposition—an exposition with a second tonality between the tonic and dominant—may appear somewhat mystifying. If an exposition is a polarization of tonic and dominant (or tonic and mediant), how does the third key enter the scheme? And how can such a scheme escape being necessarily less effective?

The answers are mostly simple, although no single answer is valid for all cases. The three-key exposition first appears in the last decade of the eighteenth century as a manifestation of the expansion of all musical forms of that time.[3] Examples continue to appear more frequently from 1800 on.

3. A very early example is in Haydn's Quartet in D major, op. 17 no. 6 of 1771; but that comes as a result of the old-fashioned practice of starting the second group with the dominant minor. (See above, p. 154) The harmonic scheme there results in: I v VII♭ V, or D major, A minor, C major (this last for thirteen bars, 40–53), A major. The C major is only a variant of the A minor, a more dramatic coloring.

A general rule can be given, however, for the earliest experiments: the second key is not fully established, and it is conceived above all in its relation to the dominant that will follow. Beethoven's Piano Sonata in D major, op. 10 no. 3 (1796–98), shows this quite simply; the counterstatement initiates the first modulation:

One of the most common ways of going from I to V was through the relative minor: V of vi to vi, V of V to V (see above p. 235). This example simply makes the process take a little longer than usual: a pause on V of vi (fermata in bar 22); a new theme on vi (bar 23); a move to V of V (V⁷ of V in bar 35) approached through the dominant minor (F♯) of vi (B minor) setting up a sequential movement; and V in bar 37—with a little more conventional effort to make this more solid by introducing the V of V of V in bar 46. It is very well done, but there are no surprises; we merely stop on the road to V.

Later examples from Beethoven are more interesting. The same progression can be used, interpolating the dominant minor into the move to V of V to V. In G major we would have:

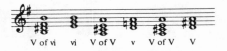

Then the dominant minor is enlarged by the following inner expansion:[4]

leading to B♭ major, which Beethoven seizes upon in the Piano Concerto no. 4 in G major. The solo part alone will suffice to show how this parenthesis is turned into a lyric section.

4. See my *Classical Style* for a longer discussion of the essential classical technique: the inner expansion of a phrase (pp. 83–89 and 279–82).

The B♭ major of bars 105 to 109 is essentially an expressive appoggiatura to the A (V of V), as a glance at the bass line will show.

This process is carried further in the Piano Concerto no. 5 in E♭ major (the *Emperor*), but it has become more complex, and we shall need the full score, as the orchestration helps to clarify the harmonic technique. The progression is E♭, B major (B minor, C♭ major), B♭ major—and one might think that the preceding technique of an appoggiatura to V of V had been daringly extended as an appoggiatura to the dominant itself, but that is not what happens:

The basic progression, before expansion, is a simple one, and like the example from the Concerto in G major, creates a Neapolitan relationship to V of V, a G♭ appoggiatura to an F:

The expansion for the third key (B major) lies between bars 133 and 164: and the third "key" is not a key at all but a magnificent prolongation by a series of 6/4 chords of the G♭ major triad (which is not a key either, but a step in the progression from E♭ major to B♭ major through the tonic minor once again). The expansion goes:

Two things are immediately evident from the score: the F♯-G♭ is the most prominent note, and it is generally the lowest note of each phrase (remark the relentless repetition of G♭-F♯ not only in bars 133 to 147 but as a kind of insistent interior pedal in bars 148 to 157). As a consequence, each phrase resolves into an F♯-major triad, which is the fundamental point of rest harmonically throughout. B minor-C♭ major is never established, but kept in an unstable, although wonderfully controlled, relation to the F♯ triad first played in bar 133. Everything else prolongs that triad until it is resolved into the 6/4 of B♭ major on the last beat of bar 163.

The stroke of genius is in bars 156–58: it is one of the most magical effects in all Beethoven, creating an aura of distance, a sudden opening out of space. Here, if anywhere, there is an illusion of resolution into the key of C♭ major (with the C♭ for one moment at last the lowest note of the phrase)—but the magic comes precisely from its being an illusion. This phrase like every other one is resolved again (bar 163) into an F♯-major triad. The instrumentation shows us how it is done. The C♭ is held by the pedal in the solo part; the double-bass only plays pizzicato. Throughout this phrase the everpresent G♭ of the entire expansion is softly sustained by a solo cello. At bar 159, the G♭ becomes, after all, the lowest note of the phrase, and everything is resolved into its triad at 163. (The F plays the same role in what follows, as the next phrase similarly resolves to the F major or V of V.)

In short, this immense execursion to C♭ is a projection and prolongation of a G♭ dissonant to the F. It was necessary to quote at such length, because this passage is perhaps the largest such expansion within a sonata form, and the way it is sustained shows the range that the style could achieve.

Schubert's practice is both more complex and more daring. The great C-major Quintet, written in the last year of his life, appears to interpose E♭ major between C major and G major, and the "Second Group" goes directly without warning to E♭ after a half-cadence on V of the tonic minor:

But the return to C major without warning in bar 71 shows that the status of Eb major is not that of an established opposing tonality to C, but a contrast of color. What is unusual here is that G major is established by the second theme itself, a procedure used by Mozart in the Viola Quintet in G minor, K. 516 (see p. 239). Schubert's progression is an expansion of the most ordinary cadence:

The theme is a way of delaying the cadence by lingering in a chromatic region, oscillating between Eb major and G major: neither are fully treated as tonalities until the G major is established by the cadence at the end of the phrase. Before that the G-major chord is still the dominant of C, felt as C minor because of the Eb harmony with which the theme opens. The secret of Schubert's wonderful color effect is that the Eb major is still only a chromatic harmony in another tonality, but it is treated for a brief moment as if it were a key in its own right. The sweetness of this theme has its source in the ambiguity, the attempt to sustain what is essentially transient. That is why the sudden C-major chord of bar 71 has the effect of a sentiment for which it is difficult to find the exact words, but which implies both renunciation and acceptance, a return to what was always intended.[5]

5. In a fine article, "Schubert's Sonata Form and Brahms' First Maturity" in *Nineteenth-Century Music*, vol. II, 1 (1978), pp. 18–35, James Webster writes (p. 29) that the

Some of the analytical ambiguity may be resolved by taking a slightly larger view of this passage. The previous phrase ends in the minor mode, with a half-cadence on G as the dominant of C minor. The Eb harmony then resolves naturally back to that same dominant of C minor in bar 64, and surprisingly melts into C major. The basic modulation is then a very simple one, the dominant now established in an all-too-familiar fashion:

with a doubly exotic coloring. The C minor is first transformed into its relative major, Eb, and then into its own major mode, C major, before being allowed to proceed. Schubert's play with major-minor relationships is obsessive at the end of his life, and it is at its most masterly here.

The *tour de force* of Schubert's way of handling the three-key exposition is the last piano sonata in Bb major. The structure is:

First theme:	A	Bb major	bars	1–18
	B	Gb major		19–35
	A	Bb major		36–47
Second group:		F# minor	⟶	F major

The second tonality, F# minor, is prepared by the ternary structure of the first theme with its central section in Gb major. The return of Bb major in the first theme is on a dominant pedal; it serves in this way itself as a bridge passage:

"mediant Eb is thus not a key but a gigantic floating pivot chord." I think that the extraordinary reappearance of C major in bar 71 and the way it is sustained make "pivot chord" an inadequate description of the way the new theme in Eb acts. With a pivot chord, we should find one tonality on one side and the new one on the other; indeed, the Eb ought, by rights, to be a pivot chord, but the return to C major erodes its function. It is this doubly ambiguous status of the harmony that gives such poignance to this section.

The dominant pedal is sustained throughout bars 36–45. The relationship of the F♯ minor that follows to the F major is more complex than the examples from Beethoven. The subsidiary movements are more numerous and the continual swing back and forth between F♯ and F ♮ (or E♯) in the bass less straightforward. It is easy enough to discern the basic progression, but difficult to reduce it to a diagram without doing a profound injustice to the wonderfully expressive ambiguities of the surface. The reader may have the pleasure of working it out, by playing over the passage, noticing the way that A major appears, only to be immediately inflected and weakened by the B♭ in the bass (bars 58–59), the suggestion of B minor that is never carried out, and the new harmonic meaning of D minor attached briefly to the F♮ in the bass but sustained so briefly. The unity of the whole progression depends on the following frame[6], in which the parallel harmonic movement before and after the new theme indicates that the section in F♯ minor is a magnificent detour:

The opening phrase of the first theme of this movement ends with a trill in the bass, *pianissimo,* on a G♭ resolved into an F, and the more one plays it, the more the entire work seems to arise out of that mysterious sonority. The long passage in F♯ minor works out the implications of the opening theme on the largest scale.

6. The same basic progression that underlies this passage had been used a few years before in another of Schubert's three-key expositions, that of the Grand Duo. The intermediate key—between tonic and dominant—is arrived at by suddenly transposing everything up a half step and then back down again.

The second tonality in the exposition of the *Lebensstürme* allegro movement for four hands of 1828 is framed by parallel modulations in an even more striking way. These parallelisms reduce the polarized energy of the expositions by turning the opposition of tonalities into a sequential movement. It is in this that Schubert's influence on later generations is most powerful.

X Ⅻ   Development

THE WORD DEVELOPMENT has two meanings which partly overlap: it indicates both the "central" section of a sonata, and a series of techniques of thematic transformation. The functions of a development section are, in fact, not peculiar to it and may be distributed over both the exposition and recapitulation (and even taken up by a coda).

The techniques of thematic transformation are 1) fragmentation; 2) deformation; 3) use of themes (or fragments) in an imitative contrapuntal texture; 4) transposition and arrangement in a rapidly modulating sequence. The texture created is generally characterized by periods shorter than in the opening of the exposition and may even contain broken or irregular sets of periods; the harmonic motion is naturally faster than that of the more stable sections.

The three main places in a sonata movement where development is most likely to occur are: 1) the modulation to V in the exposition (when the exposition is in three parts, the developmental techniques will be much in evidence in the central section); 2) the so-called development section proper; 3) the second phrase or thereabouts of the recapitulation, which often initiates the secondary development section. The texture is also sometimes found in the coda, and Mozart often employed it to vary the second group in such works as the E-major Trio, K. 542, where the dominant (B major) section of the exposition modulates as far as G minor.

The central section of a sonata form has two separate functions, development and retransition: the development intensifies the polarization and delays resolution; the retransition prepares the resolution. As late as 1791, Koch considerd the modulation of the retransition back to I as an appendix to the central section, and it is indeed often a short, completely separate section.

In the second half of the eighteenth century the development section most often began with the main theme played at the dominant and ended with a cadence on the relative minor. (Both stereotypes were felt to be tedious and old-fashioned by the end of the century; neither of them was ever abandoned.) After the cadence on vi, there was either a retransition or the recapitulation followed without further ado. The development in the first movement of Johann Christian Bach's Symphony in D major, op. 18 no. 4 (published in 1781), illustrates the separation between development and retransition. The development starts at bar 51; it opens not with the main theme, but with a new theme:

55 PREMATURE REPRISE

The cadence on vi in bar 71 is decisive enough. The opening of this section shows the form of the "premature reprise" even with new material, as the new material is first played at V (bars 51–54) and then immediately at I, demonstrating once again that this stereotype (type 2 of our aria forms) had its harmonic charms which were independent of the thematic structure.

One way of escaping the eternal cadence on vi preceding the return to I—or at least enlivening it—was by a cadence on V of vi, followed by a jump into the tonic and the main theme. Michael Haydn's Symphony in E♭ major of 1783 has a rather grand example of this with a dramatic effect:

His brother Joseph used it, too, several times. One of the most beautiful examples is in the Kyrie of the *Harmoniemesse* of 1802, perhaps his liturgical masterpiece. The Kyrie is in sonata form, poco adagio, and the end of the development is:

The cadence on vi (G minor) is neatly avoided. The laconic return which makes the reprise of the main theme and a full tutti so powerful and so moving is accomplished by the three rising notes in violas, cellos, and basses without continuo.

One could compile a large anthology from 1770 on of ways to avoid a cadence on vi at the end of the development. Mozart's technique, as one would expect, is the most accomplished. The end of the development of the Symphony in Eb major, K. 543, is perhaps the most brilliant example:

The cadence stops short one chord away from resolution: one bar of silence is substituted for vi; three bars of retransition lead at once to the reprise.

Perhaps the wittiest use of this movement from V of vi to the recapitulation is in Muzio Clementi's Sonata in D major, op. 40 no. 3 (published 1802), an effect as poetic as it is ingenious:

Clementi pretends that there will be a firm cadence on vi, and produces the conventional trill to induce belief. Then he switches the harmony to V⁷ of I in bar 175, and proceeds with the recapitulation.

Going from V of vi to I is, as Clementi shows us, an ellipse. The original form of full cadence on vi followed by retransition, however brief, remains the original model. It is Mendelssohn who makes the most striking use of it. The Overture to the *Midsummer Night's Dream* opens:

The development ends with a cadence on vi (C♯ minor), a cadence of complete exhaustion. With Mendelssohn, the end of the development is often not a climax but the lowest point of tension.

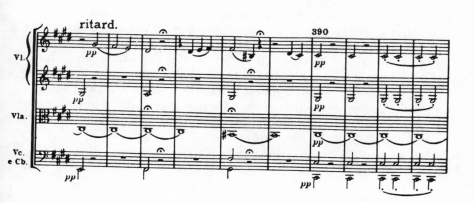

The E-major return has the simplicity of genius: the E and G# of the flutes are placed over the C# of the strings, who then retire. The return is out of phase; the main theme returns before the tonic harmony, and it is the theme itself which forms the retransition. It needs only four bars.

The development section can take over not only some of the functions of the recapitulation, but even those of the exposition. This is valid, above all, for what I have called minuet sonata form. See, for example, the scherzo from Schubert's Piano Sonata in A major (1828), in which the motifs of the first phrase are rearranged at the beginning of the second part to create an entirely new pattern. This is, of course, a common procedure. The minuet of Beethoven's Sonata in D major, op. 10 no. 3, provides another good example:

After the double bar, there is clearly both a second group and a development, that is, new material oriented to the dominant area (the modulation is our familiar way of arriving at the dominant, V of vi to vi, V of V to V,) and a developmental texture, fragmented, sequential, and contrapuntal. There are many examples of new material introduced in the development section; Beethoven's *Eroica* is the most famous example, although here the new material is related to the main theme. We must distinguish in eighteenth-century practice between development sections which introduce a characteristic and memorable new theme into the thematic development of material drawn from the exposition, and those which make no allusion to the exposition whatever. In the latter scheme, represented by Mozart's Sonata for Piano in C major, K. 330, no new theme of pronounced character appears, and the material is loosely related—above all by rhythmic contour—to the exposition. Here, however, one cannot speak of thematic development.

The texture of the development section generally resembles Baroque texture more than any other part of a sonata: it must avoid both the decisive modulation of the exposition and the stability of the recapitulation, essential inventions of sonata style. To this end, not only the contrapuntal imitative texture but also the sequential movement of the Baroque are employed (sequences involving a descent from iii to ii are most common in the eighteenth century). The modulations must not only be rapid, but must also never give the impression of a second tonality as strong as the dominant; some kind of sequential motion —which implies further movement with no necessary or logical stopping place—is most useful. The chromaticism of the development section is almost always more pronounced than in any other for the same reason—to postpone stability.

The sequential structure of the development is the most important aspect for the nineteenth century. The sequence is enormously expanded by Schubert, a technique adopted by Bruckner. In Schubert's Piano Trio in E♭ major, D. 929 (1827), one of the themes is presented in the development section in a series of sequences lasting fifty-two bars; then the entire fifty-two bars is repeated, transposed up a fifth. The whole series begins for a third time, but in the middle a chromatic alteration turns the passage into a retransition and leads us back to the tonic and the main theme. In short, Schubert arranges sequences sequentially. This large-scale rhythmical organization is related to the eight-bar period so often imposed on the musical flow throughout the nineteenth century like a slow beat that controls the flow. (The fifty-two bar sequence in the Trio is, in fact, arranged as six eight-bar phrases, with two extra bars both before and after the first phrase.)

The relation that Strunk makes (see p. 156) between the false reprise and the mid-century pattern of starting the development with the main theme played first at V and then at I ("premature reprise") is reasonable only when dealing with works as short as the baritone trios of the early 1760s. We may accept the tendentious term "premature reprise" for the stereotype, as there is no point in multiplying terminology. A false reprise, however, is intended to fool the listener, or at least to surprise him, and nobody can have been surprised by this all-too-commonplace but soon-to-be-obsolete device. We can clear the matter up, at least in part, by taking an extreme case: the first movement of Haydn's Symphony in E♭ major, no. 55, of 1774 has a "premature reprise," a "false reprise," a "real reprise," and, to start with, a pun on the idea of reprise. We need to see the opening bars of the exposition to understand the sequence of events in the development:

The exposition ends with the opening motif of the four repeated chords and the development begins with it now moving to the relative minor:

The pun is in bars 69–70: they recapitulate bars 3–4 at the right pitch but in the wrong context. After the repeated chords (V^7 of vi), the main theme at the tonic pitch but not in the tonic harmony is one of Haydn's fine strokes of humor. It prepares the immediate appearance of the "premature reprise" which Haydn had largely abandoned by 1774 but which he has a use for now as it will make his false reprise all the more false—that is, all the more convincing. The "premature reprise" starts in bar 73 with the oboe doubling; it is over by bar 78 when the move to IV begins, only to be cut short at once by a turn to iii. The harmony settles firmly on V of iii in bar 84 and from there, the closing theme is used to move gradually through a dozen bars back to the tonic.

The return to the tonic is the occasion for the false reprise in bar 97. This starts with the opening motto and continues with the main theme. It is over by bar 103, and like the premature reprise turns first to IV. Most of the first audience must have been fooled by this reprise, thinking, with an uneasy feeling, that the development had been much too short. The humor still gives pleasure after many hearings.

The rest of the development is unconventional in its proportions; it has a conventional final cadence on vi in bar 123 which is followed by a very long retransition. So long, in fact, that much of it must be counted as additional development—but then Haydn was accustomed to add development wherever he pleased. Bars 123 to 150 are a tonic preparation: the establishment of I is already achieved by bar 139 and ten bars are then spent in making the return of the opening seem inevitable. The real reprise starts at bar 151.

A false reprise is not only a false resolution, but a brief moment of consonance in the most dissonant section of the work. The development section prolongs the tension set up by the exposition above all because much of the dissonance of the work is concentrated in its center. This is reinforced by the rapidity and the instability of the modulations as the music moves through a variety of keys, many of them only glanced at and never confirmed. The false reprise is a false repose: both the way it enters and the way it disappears are conceived as shocks, as both come too soon.

Perhaps nothing demonstrates the efficacy and the powers of the sonata style better than the ability to increase tension by a false moment of stasis. The false reprise is only a specialized and not very supple form of this. More interesting is the arrest of the movement in the development section of Haydn's Piano Trio in E major (H. XV:28). The opening theme:

appears towards the beginning of the development transformed:

This is not a false reprise. If a reprise is not in the tonic (or the sub-dominant), it fools only the uneducated, and I doubt if this one would fool anybody into thinking that the recapitulation had begun. In its force and stability, it calls a sudden halt to the development, and therefore implies that it will be followed by increased movement and energy.

The most brilliant use before Beethoven of these static moments that generate tension may be found in more than ten bars of a repeated drone bass and a continuous *forte* that prepare the recapitulation in Haydn's *Emperor* Quartet in C major, op. 76 no. 3:

This is so relentless that Haydn did not need to bother with a modulation to C major: he changes the G♯ to G♮, keeps the pedal on E through another four bars *pianissimo*, and brings in the main theme in the tonic. The C major is reestablished convincingly simply by virtue of the relief that it brings after fourteen bars of an unchanging and insistent pedal point.

Beethoven's use of this apparent repose in a development section is on too large a scale to deal with here. Perhaps the most moving example of it may be found in the development of the first movement of the String Quartet in B♭ major, op. 130, with its soft ostinato motion under the lyrical phrases of the first violin. It is Schubert, however, who made the effect most personal.

XI ⅃⅃　　　Recapitulation

THE PRINCIPLE OF *recapitulation as resolution* may be considered the most fundamental and radical innovation of sonata style. The germ of this conception may be found in the Baroque binary forms, but the sonata does not, like the binary forms, merely repeat all or part of the exposition now transposed into the tonic (with or without variations). In the sonata there is a *reinterpretation* of the pattern of the exposition, a transformation of a clearly articulated movement away from stability into the affirmation of a large stable area.

The principles of reinterpretation, of resolution, need defining. Theorists of the eighteenth century and later have traditionally paid less attention to the recapitulation than to other sections of the sonata—giving, in the eighteenth century, the impression that the composer was free to do much as he liked, and, in the nineteenth, that the repetition of the opening material was a cut-and-dried affair. Even in the nineteenth century, however, this section exhibits as great a variety of forms as the exposition and development.

What must be emphasized first of all is that the form of the recapitulation is determined as much by the development section as by the exposition on which it is more obviously based. The greater the dramatic tension created by the development, the more elaborate the measures taken in the recapitulation to resolve that tension. The recapitulation may, to this end, continue the thematic development while resolving the harmonic tensions.

284

The traditional name for this section is a misnomer (as are the German *Reprise* and the French *réexposition*); in continuing to use the term recapitulation we must not assume that the eighteenth-century composer was required to begin at the head with the first theme, or that he had to go over the whole of the exposition. Indeed, it was possible to begin anywhere in the first group.

Returning to the tonic with bar 3 or bar 5 of the opening is a stereotype of the middle of the eighteenth century that derives, as I have said, from the reprise of the aria type 3. Often it was done perfunctorily. It must have satisfied a loose sense of symmetry: bars 1–4 at the beginning of the development, bar 5 and what follows at the opening of the recapitulation. At any rate the formula appears to have given satisfaction for more than a generation, and in many countries.

Great effects could be wrung from it by a composer with a sense of drama. C. P. E. Bach made perhaps the most effective use. The finale of the Sonata in F♯ minor[1] demonstrates that this device can have great power. The opening bars are:

---

1. No. IV from *Zweyte Fortsetzung von Sechs Sonaten fürs Clavier*, Berlin, 1763. I am indebted to Darrell Berg for a copy of this work.

The return begins with bar 3 at the tonic after the first two bars have appeared in D major:

The sudden halt in bar 67, followed by a bar's silence, and the return, marked *piano*, are both forceful and subtle, and very moving. It is easy to see why Haydn said he learnt everything from Philip Emanuel Bach.

Later in the century it was still possible to avoid playing the opening bars at the start of the recapitulation, but then it was generally necessary to bring them back at the end. Mozart, in the Piano Sonata in D major, K. 311 (1778), begins his recapitulation just before the second group, reserving the first theme for the close. There are many examples of this recapitulation in reverse or mirror form: we find it in Mozart's Violin Sonata in D major, K. 306 (1778); in the great quartet no. 21 of *Idomeneo* (1780); and in the Symphony in C major, K. 338 (also 1780). Haydn uses it in the finale of Symphony no. 44 in E minor (ca. 1772)[2] and Clementi in his Sonata in G major, op. 39 no. 2 (1798).

The rarity of this form after 1780 marks an important change in so-

2. See also the remarks above on the *Hornsignal* Symphony, p. 224 ff.

nata style between the 1750s and the 1780s. It is not so much that recapitulations beginning with the first theme had practically become the rule rather than only the most common form, but that a direct correlation between the thematic and tonal structures is now made possible by the new conception of the theme as the bearer of highly individualized and immediately identifiable interlocking motifs. The possibility of a partial identification of the tonic with the opening themes naturally becomes greater and more urgent as the opening theme is more "characteristic" (in the sense that the word was used in the eighteenth and nineteenth centuries, meaning "idiosyncratic, expressive, full of character").

This does not imply that, by the 1780s, the order of the material in the exposition was always retained in the recapitulation. In the case of an exposition which uses the first theme again to begin the second group, or which contains an extensive and elaborate modulation to the dominant, this order is clearly difficult to repeat without considerable alteration. The changes made in the material in the recapitulation are rarely decorative; they have a structural meaning. What must reappear in the recapitulation—and this is a rule that holds true from the very beginnings of anything that can be called sonata style—is the second group, at least any part of it that has an individual and characteristic aspect, and that does not already have its analogue in the first group. The resolution of this material confirms the articulation of the exposition into stable and dissonant sections. A theme that has been played only at the dominant is a structural dissonance, unresolved until it has been transposed to the tonic.[3]

3. In an interesting review of the first edition of this book in *Music Analysis* (I: 2, p. 218), David Osmond-Smith comments about this sentence: "We will more readily take it as a description of how we perceive, or at least can be taught to perceive large-scale structure, than as an observation, couched in perceptual metaphor, about an idea that has provoked composers into creative activity." This seems to me deeply mistaken. It should be clear that at least for some eighteenth-century composers—Mozart, above all—resolution at a distance is important whether or not it can be perceived. The rule that the finale of a Mozart opera, for example, must begin and end in the same key is only true after Mozart is seventeen years old. I do not believe that either his hearing or the sensitivity of his perception suddenly improved at that age. He had obviously made certain decisions about aesthetic balance at that time. It is true that one can be taught to hear much of this resolution at a distance, but we must not dismiss too easily the notion that the tonal balance is beautiful in conception even if sometimes difficult to perceive in actual practice, and it would be foolish to overlook the influence of this kind of theory. It is in fact a basic problem for a composer to ascertain how much of this balance can be made easily perceptible to a listener, and certainly Mozart and Beethoven went farther than any others to make this effect audible. We may not demand the recapitulation, but it ends by satisfying us. I do not, however, believe that one can claim to be immediately conscious of every aspect of this long-distance resolution, and I do not share the prejudice that this consciousness is absolutely desirable.

This is less a compositional canon, therefore, than a sense of the aesthetic balance essential to late eighteenth-century style. In the few cases where it appears to be broken, either the theme of the second group which does not appear in the recapitulation is replaced there by a passage of significantly similar harmonic character and shape (e.g., Haydn's Symphony no. 75, where bars 52–55 are represented harmonically by 135–40), or else the theme has already appeared *at the tonic* in the development section, as in the first movement of J. C. Bach's Symphony in E♭ major op. 9 no. 2, or Haydn's Quartet in G major, op. 77 no. 1. In the latter example, the theme serves to prepare and reestablish the tonic, and the development section has accordingly taken over part of the function of resolution. The same observation may be made of Mozart's Piano Sonata in C minor, K. 457, of 1784: one of the themes of the second group never reappears in the recapitulation, but has been played in the development section at the subdominant. This is also a clear indication of the role of the subdominant in the Viennese classical language: it possesses some of the resolving function of the tonic.

On the other hand, when the development contains new material, it, too, may be resolved in the recapitulation. This does not apply to new material immediately and obviously related to one of the principal themes of the exposition, as in Mozart's Sonata for Piano in F major, K. 332, but to material of a character evidently very different from anything in the exposition. The development of Mozart's Sonata for Two Pianos, K. 375a(448), opens with a new theme at the dominant and it is accordingly resolved at the end of the recapitulation; the new theme at the dominant that begins the development of the first movement of Mozart's Piano Concerto in A major, K. 488, also reappears in the recapitulation at the tonic.

In finales—whether in rondo form or not—we sometimes find new material introduced in the development in the subdominant (for example, the finale of Mozart's Sonata in F major, K. 332, which has no other characteristics of the rondo. See page 131.) Such material needs no resolution. The subdominant plays a special role in sonata style; it acts itself as a force for resolution, an antidominant, in fact, and there is a tendency for the second half of a sonata to move toward the subdominant and the related flat keys. There even arose a kind of degenerate recapitulation, which began not in the tonic but in the subdominant, and which made possible a literal reprise of the exposition, transposed down a fifth. The best-known example of that is the little Piano Sonata in C major of Mozart, K. 545, but it exists almost from the beginning of the sonata forms (see above p. 144). It was taken up enthusiastically by Schubert, who used it in many of the early works.[4] A more interesting role of the subdominant, however, is in the Secondary Development section, where it is, in fact, the generating force.

The Secondary Development section appears in the great majority of late eighteenth-century works soon after the beginning of the recapitulation and often with the second phrase. Sometimes it is only a few bars long, sometimes very extensive indeed. The purpose of this section is to lower harmonic tension without sacrificing interest; it introduces an allusion to the subdominant or to the related "flat" keys. This use of IV was familiar to eighteenth-century theorists. Koch, in his description of the recapitulation, calls attention to it; he also insists on the absence of a cadence in IV, which implies that the modulation must be introduced as part of a section of developmental character. Koch also recommends the abbreviation of the first group ("die vorzüglichsten Sätze werden nun gleichsam zusammen gedrängt") and the full return of the thematic content of the second group ("endlich wird die zweyte Hälfte des ersten Perioden, diejenigen melodischen Theile des ersten Perioden, die dem Quintabsätze in der Quinte folgten, in dieser Hauptonart wiederholt").[5]

It would be a mistake to identify the appearance of the subdominant in the Secondary Development section with the necessary alteration of harmony to transform an exposition that goes from tonic to dominant into a recapitulation that remains in the tonic. The Secondary Development as often as not returns to one of the themes of the *first* group, which necessitates a still further change later in the section in order to bring the second group into the tonic. Beethoven's *Waldstein* Sonata gives us a simple example. Between the return of bars 12 and 14 of the exposition:

4. For a massive recapitulation starting at IV, see Hummel's Piano Trio in E♭ major, op. 96, sometimes also labeled op. 93.

5. H. C. Koch, *Versuch einer Anleitung zur Composition*, Leipzig, 1793, III, p. 311.

the recapitulation interpolates a short development in the flat or sub-dominant direction:

This introduction of the subdominant area (D♭ major, E♭ major, and C minor) serves to make the return of the tonic more decisive.[6] It is the restoration of harmonic equilibrium as well as the need for variation that gives the Secondary Development its function.

Since, theoretically at least, all works of sonata style are written in a harmonic system of equal temperament, a subdominant or dominant key is not an absolute; going around the circle of fifths in the dominant direction will soon lead into the subdominant area, and vice versa. A key relationship is therefore defined by how it is approached.

This may be demonstrated most easily by an extreme case, a famous passage of Secondary Development in which Beethoven turns a dominant key into a subdominant one. The passage is the opening of the reprise of the *Eroica* Symphony, where the C♯ in the cellos is interpreted now as if it were a D♭ and leads to a new development:

6. I have given several earlier examples of Secondary Development sections above, notably pages 108–10 and 176.

In this new development the main theme is played in the supertonic (F major), the flatted leading tone (Db major), and finally on V⁷ of I.

The F major, however, is approached as if it were going to be F minor: the major mode of bar 409 is a surprise, as the preceding progression implies a movement to ii, the relative minor of the subdominant. Not for a moment, in fact, is the F major heard as if it were V of V, which is what it would be if approached as a dominant instead of as a chromatic coloring of the subdominant; not for a moment does the music suggest that the F major will lead to Bb major. The subdominant is confirmed by what follows: the return to a Db, now a tonality, Db major. The sense of the harmonic shift may be seen if we look at the key relations:

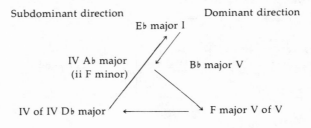

The progression moves apparently to ii (F minor) changing to V of V (F major) at the last moment; it then compensates by moving to IV of IV (the subdominant of the subdominant, Db major), and resolves back to I through V⁷.

These details, tedious though they may be on paper, partly account for the illusionistic color of the F-major/Dᵇ-major sequences, perhaps the supreme example of Beethoven's handling of local, small-scale tonal relations. The contradiction of the normal significance of V of V, its transformation into its opposite, makes this moment one in which all genuine harmonic motion appears to stop: the dynamics, *piano* and *dolce*, reflect the cessation of harmonic energy. The main theme is poised over these harmonies for a few bars. This is a crucial passage: the main theme is essentially a horn call in its character, but the horn has yet to play it solo. The second horn tried to, a few bars before, in Eᵇ, but was cut off brutally in mid-theme by the full orchestra. The first horn plays the theme at last, but with a different sonority—not the long-expected sonority of Eᵇ major; he changes to an instrument in F, the supertonic. The swift move to Dᵇ major, and the delicacy of the flute solo confirm the exoticism of this section.

Most secondary developments, however, go without any trouble to the subdominant. In fact, throughout the later eighteenth century in almost all large forms—opera aria, concerto, sonata, symphony—the move to IV soon after the opening of the reprise is a kind of second nature. The coherence of the system depended on it. On the rare occasions when it is entirely omitted, either there has been so heavy an emphasis on IV in the development that anything further would be pleonastic, or the omission is made up later—as in Beethoven's Piano Sonata in Eᵇ major, op. 31 no. 3, where the coda opens with the first theme in IV.

The recapitulation often depends on the possibility of rearranging the elements of the exposition in a different order, and drawing new meaning from the new arrangement. I have given an example of expository elements used at the end of a retransition to reintroduce the tonic in Mozart's "Prague" Symphony on page 201ff, and a similar example may be found in Beethoven's Quartet in F major, op. 59 no. 1. The first movement opens with three clearly distinct sections:

A

All these characterize the main key leisurely and emphatically. When they return later, they have a different order and a different significance

Section B returns after a dominant pedal at the end of the development, and it serves here to hold off, as well as prepare, the full return and to justify the beautiful effect when the first violin is out of phase by one bar as the cello begins the main theme, and section A is replayed. Section C is used for a secondary development, as well as to complete the move to the subdominant or flat area already initiated at the end of the main theme. Eliminating the bass at the opening of this section gives it an exquisitely delicate sound which makes the mark of *dolce* more intense.

The proportions of the final area of stability (i.e., the recapitulation and coda) have structural significance. What follows the return to the tonic that initiates the recapitulation takes up about one-quarter of the whole movement. In the case of an unusually lengthy development, therefore, an extension of the recapitulation by excursions into the subdominant or by a coda is inevitable in the work of any composer with sensibility, and a feeling for the expressive values of the style. The clearest manifestation of this new sense of proportions is the increasing importance given to the length of the final cadence.

XII   Codas

THE APPEARANCE of a coda always disturbs the binary symmetry of a
sonata form. It establishes a different kind of balance. The symmetry of
the different binary structures that were transformed into sonatas is most
evident at the end of the two sections: the parallelism of the conclusions
of each part is generally very faithful. While the opening of each section
is often varied, and what follows hard upon the opening of the second
part is most often radically different from the first, our sense of the equilibrium of sonata style depends on the conformity of the endings. This
conformity is disrupted by the appearance of a coda. One might say that
the coda is a sign of dissatisfaction with the form, a declaration in each
individual case that the symmetry is inadequate to the demands of the
material, that the simple parallelism has become constraining.

There are essentially two kinds of codas: those that appear as a completely separate postscript to the second part after this has been repeated;
and, somewhat less frequent, those that are placed at the end of the
second part, but within the indications for repetition. In the latter case,
indeed, the coda may sometimes be found before the concluding bars
which parallel the end of the exposition or part one, and this restores
the traditional symmetry. Of course, when the indications for repeating
the second section vanish, as they so often do in the last years of the
eighteenth century, this distinction becomes uninteresting and metaphysical, but before that time it is very real. Both kinds appear simultaneously in 1769.

297

It is in the set of quartets op. 9 by Haydn that we first find a coda attached to movements we can call sonata forms without discomfort. It will be more than a decade before we find anything comparable in the symphonies or piano sonatas. Haydn begins timidly. The finale of opus 9 no. 5 in B♭ major has a coda in which the final bars of the form are merely repeated, like the reprise of the last phrase so often found in the music of Couperin and his contemporaries. However—as always with Haydn—there is a difference. The end of the second part before the coda repeats not only the end of the first part, but also the beginning of the second part, with an effect of great wit:

END OF FIRST PART

END OF SECOND PART AND CODA

and this leaves us with a dissonance hanging in the air; the coda is necessary to round off the joke. (There is a pleasant example of Haydn's wit in the way the second violin in bars 194 to 198 plays the first violin's line of bars 77–80.) It is clear that this coda is not, like a simple reprise, a luxury, but a necessity.

The very short finale of the quartet that follows, op. 9 no. 6 in A major, has a coda which is indeed an extravagant luxury. This movement is a simple three-phrase binary form, but it is worth examining here briefly, as the coda is the result of forces similar to those that created sonata style, and it will help us to establish the principles by which the classical coda is constructed. First and third phrases on the tonic are similar although ingeniously varied (bars 1–8 and 25–32), and the second phrase establishes the dominant (bars 9–20); a four-bar retransition follows (bars 21–24):

The piece is over at bar 32, but the coda, in one of Haydn's most humor-ous inspirations, seems unwilling to let it end, and adds a series of four-bar phrases which sound surprisingly irregular and abrupt. We must, as always, look to the main body of the piece to understand this coda. Before the coda there are essentially three eight-bar phrases and a four-bar retransition between phrases two and three, but a striking irregular-ity has been built into the second phrase, which has been turned into a twelve-bar phrase by the insertion of bars 14–17; the underlying form would skip from bar 13 to 18 with no difficulty, as bars 14–17 merely keep repeating the pattern of bar 13 and anticipating bar 18; they only serve to prevent progress. The insertion, if perfectly standard, is a delightful one. The coda picks up the same technique and similarly pro-longs the final cadence beyond anyone's reasonable expectations. The indication to repeat could have been placed after the opening of bar 32, leaving the coda as a separate section, but Haydn evidently liked it well enough to hear it twice. In any case, we may begin to suspect that the classical coda is closely related to an anomaly in the main body of the work.

Opus 17, written two years later, will confirm this. The finales of no. 1 in E major, a full-fledged sonata form this time, has a twenty-four-bar coda that is directly inspired by the most curious feature of the movement, the subsidiary theme of bars 19–27:

This motif appears here only at the subdominant, although in the tonic area, which is already odd enough. It returns next in the development during the all-too-standard move to the relative minor:

It is at the same pitch as in the exposition: nothing changes except its context, and therefore its function. What makes the coda necessary is that this motif does not appear again in the recapitulation. Here is the end of the formal structure and the coda:

The music seems to end in bar 214, but after a short pause we realize there is unfinished business. Bars 12–26 of the exposition come back, still at the subdominant, but then in a swift stroke in bar 231 the motif is brought down to the tonic, and bars 232–236 let us hear it properly resolved. This seems wonderfully simple, but to have conceived it implies a sensitivity to complex tonal matters.

The purpose of a coda is, if we take a common-sense attitude, to add weight and seriousness: like an introduction, it promotes dignity. It must, however, be tied even more closely to the main structure than an introduction—at least when it is attached to a sonata; an aria, on the other hand, may be completed by a *cabaletta* with which it has no material in common—but this is a different aesthetic (and in the latter half of the eighteenth century it is the sonata aesthetic that largely rules the aria). From its inception, the sonata coda was based on the material of the main structure, and was responsive to what had already happened.

This serious conception of the coda is powerfully at work in the Quartet in C minor, op. 17 no. 4, where the first-movement coda, indeed, resembles that of the first movement of Beethoven's Sonata in C minor, op. 111. To understand we must quote the opening bars:

This combines great breadth with an astonishing acceleration toward the pause in bar 8. The coda retains the sixteenth-note motion for much of its length, but the rhythm slows down gradually like a written-out *ritardando*. For a complete understanding of this beautiful page we must turn to the development and quote its most startling and dramatic moment, the unexpected frustration of the return. The dominant pedal is most emphatically prepared and established, and the phrase ends with a decisive dominant cadence, but the recapitulation is then postponed for thirteen bars:

Bar 79 seems to initiate the reprise, but instead we get an exquisite texture as yet unheard in this quartet: slow-moving, even notes, the first violin *mezzo-forte* in canon with the three other instruments *piano*, a construction that has the first violin moving in contrary motion to the other voices. This is followed, even more eccentrically but to great effect, by the main theme played at the mediant. All this holds off the return of the tonic, which finally enters, but only after bar 92 repeats bar 86 as if the main theme were to be played at the mediant once again.

The coda begins with a dramatic pause on the dominant in bar 122 similar to the one in bar 78:

This time, resolution is immediate, and symmetry is reestablished by repeating the closing theme of bars 118 and 119. The passage serves both to extend the final cadence and also to resolve the tensions left over from the development.

Haydn carries this way of thinking about the coda to the limit of complexity in the Quartet in F minor, op. 20 no. 5, perhaps the most moving and accomplished of his conclusions:

This coda is a synthesis of several crucial moments in what has preceded. The basic thematic element is the principal motif of the second group:

A return to the first bars of the development is a logical point of departure for a coda, and this second theme is substituted for the first theme at the beginning of the development:

The extraordinary harmonies and mysterious-sounding texture that follow in 142–145 are modeled on the impressive moment in the exposition which initiates the movement away from the tonic:

In the coda, all this is magnificently resolved. In bars 148–152 it is possible to hear the character and some of the outline of the opening theme of the quartet, and the coda has once again combined aspects of both first theme (see below) with the second:

If this synthesis seems small-scale, dependent on closely seen detail, that accounts for much of its intensity. The conception of the coda as a synthesis of the whole movement was to have an impressive future with Mozart and Beethoven, but from a much larger perspective. It should not be assumed that the smaller scale of Haydn's realization in this work was necessarily a disadvantage.

From this point, however, Haydn takes a longer view of the coda, which becomes, for the most part, a return to the opening bars of the movement. (Most composers use this procedure for codas—all of those that I know by Clementi, for example.) This combines a suggestion of the satisfying symmetry of ternary form, which ends where it began, with binary symmetry of the sonata—less balanced, but more dynamic. The coda essentially attempts to restore a loss of balance. We can see this at once in the codas of Haydn's Quartets op. 33. No. 3 in C major starts with a hint of the second theme:

and then takes the opening phrase

and turns it, after the standard cadential trill, into a concluding phrase by cutting off the end—here is the coda:

The reverse order—second theme, first theme—reveals the intent: a new and more effective balance.

The coda of op. 33 no. 5 (this one within the repeat signs) uses the two initial motifs of the movement in reverse order:

The theme ends in bars 9 and 10 with the initial motif, so this relationship is already established at the opening, but the coda spells it out completely. The coda begins with bar 272:

Initiating the coda with an unexpected chord (here the flatted submediant) will become a commonplace, and so will the return to the opening.

This establishes the pattern for Haydn's symphonies, which begin to exhibit codas in 1783 with no. 81 in G major. Here the opening phrase returns at the end, and the justification is that this phrase does not appear in its original form in the recapitulation, but only poetically rewritten— the coda fills a gap, as well as rounding off the form. The symphonies are naturally painted with a much larger brush than the quartets, and the recall of the opening is never subtle. The grandest of the symphonic codas are those to the last movement of no. 98 and the first movement of no. 102 (the "Drumroll"): the former begins *piu moderato* in broad cadenza style and has a solo for the continuo instrument; in the latter, the slow introduction returns, perhaps in imitation of the coda to Mozart's Viola Quintet in D major, K. 593.

The greater breadth of some of Mozart's conceptions must have influenced Haydn's later practice. The ambition of some of Mozart's codas is striking. I presume that he is the inventor of the contrapuntal coda. It is important to emphasize that these are not simple displays, but always seem to be demanded by the material. The coda of the first movement of the "Hunt" Quartet in B♭, K. 458, major presents one of the best examples:

No one should be impressed by countrapuntal imitation based on descending thirds—it is too easy to achieve; but that is just the point. With such material, the contrapuntal consequences are impossible to resist. If Mozart resists it until the coda, that is because such a structure would tear apart a Mozart exposition, even a development. (In the Sonata in Bb major, op. 106, Beethoven could manage an elaborate contrapuntal chain of descending thirds with the *fugato* section of the first movement's development, but it does not reach the density of Mozart's bars 246–253.) What is new about Mozart's coda in the "Hunt" is that it appears as the natural culmination of the movement—not just a necessary resolution but as a goal. Beethoven was to carry this even further.

It is clear, however, that Mozart often follows Haydn's lead. The coda can spring directly from an unresolved detail in the formal structure: the coda not only gives added weight, but is needed to complete what has been left undone, to add stability. In the Viola Quintet in G minor, K. 516, the main thematic element of the coda is a melody that was only heard previously as an agent of modulation:

Here in the exposition it moves up a third from G minor to B♭ major. It
modulates widely throughout the development,

and in the recapitulation it goes to the subdominant. After a wonderfully complex imitative passage, this theme returns stabilized, and even
leads the bass back to the tonic in the last bars:

Similarly, the coda of the Piano Quartet in E♭ major, K. 493, brings back the opening theme of the second group:

EXPOSITION

This serves throughout the development without cease for modulations that go from D♭ major to D minor. The reappearance in the coda is justified by its surprisingly eccentric role in the recapitulation, where it starts again in the dominant, as it was in the exposition (in spite of being preceded now by the orthodox move to the subdominant) and only subsequently moves to the tonic. It is one of Mozart's most impressive experiments with structure, achieved with a semblance of ease that is incomparable:

RECAPITULATION

After such sophistication, the coda does not need to be subtle, but uses the motif solely for an alternation of tonic and dominant harmony.

As Haydn did so often, Mozart returns to the development for his coda[1], and also seizes on an anomaly of structure to justify his expansion of form. For Mozart, as for Haydn, the coda was a logical consequence of the general conception.

The principles which generally regulate Mozart's codas are so clearly manifested in two examples that almost no word of explanation is necessary. The first movement of the Sonata for Piano and Violin in E minor, K. 304, has a main theme that appears first unharmonized, and then in a counterstatement with an expressive and contrasting accompaniment:

The recapitulation presents what is perhaps Mozart's most radical and dramatic rewriting of an opening theme:

1. Note, however, that the coda does not have the character of a development but of a cadence. We must be grateful to Professor Joseph Kerman for firmly *putting paid to* the frequent notion of the coda as further development, in his excellent and stimulating "Notes on Beethoven's Codas," in *Beethoven Studies*, 3d ed., ed. Alan Tyson, Cambridge, 1982.

It is natural that the coda should have the only absolutely simple harmonization of this melody:

This normalization of a theme is one purpose of a Mozart coda. Another is the recapitulation at the tonic of a new theme introduced in the development section; the opening allegro moderato of the Piano Sonata in C major, K. 330, provides us with the most concise example. The last four bars of the exposition and the beginning of the development are:

The theme that opens the development has not appeared previously, and it returns in a brief coda only after the exposition has been fully resolved at the tonic:

This satisfies the demands both of symmetry and harmonic resolution.

When is a coda not a coda? When it is a part of the recapitulation—which it is, essentially, throughout the eighteenth century. In the Sonata for Two Pianos, K. 375a, the return at the tonic of the new theme which opened the development, and which appeared there at the dominant, is often labeled the coda, although it is basically an acknowledgment that the development can, exceptionally, take on some of the functions of exposition: nobody then viewed the sections of a sonata as watertight compartments. And how are we to characterize these final bars of the first movement of the Piano Sonata in D, K. 311?

This is part of a "reverse" recapitulation which began with the main themes of the second group. The quotation here begins with the opening theme in bars 99–104. Bars 109–112 are the end of the exposition transposed to the tonic, but bars 105–109 are entirely new. Is this new cadential material, inserted between first theme and closing theme, to be called recapitulation or coda? It is certainly an added concluding gesture, while the last four bars reestablish a symmetry with the exposition. In general, the classical coda plays with the lopsided symmetry of a sonata form, where the emphatic return to the tonic in the middle of the second part can often act as a dynamic stimulus.

Mozart's most radical invention in the matter of codas is the finale of the "Jupiter" Symphony. Here, for the first time, the coda becomes not a postscript, but a separate section with the weight and even the length that approach the other sections of the form (both development section and coda are sixty-seven bars). This is a form that Beethoven was to appropriate, although he never attempted so elaborate a display of contrapuntal virtuosity. An aspect of the Jupiter coda which was equally influential is the way it surveys all the themes of the movement. In this case, indeed, they were all invented to combine contrapuntally in a grand synthesis, and that is interesting because it means that the movement was planned with the coda as its culmination. In this sense, Mozart goes far beyond Haydn. The coda does not, however, conclude with counterpoint but with a full reprise of bars 13–35. This is pure concerto style; these bars act in the exposition as a ritornello to begin with and return from time to time with that function, but Mozart withholds their literal reappearance in the recapitulation (a secondary development comes in their place at the right moment) and reserves them for the end.

From Mozart, Beethoven inherited the concept of the coda as a large section that can counterbalance the weight of the development and make a survey of the themes of the exposition (although, as Kerman, following Tovey, has remarked, Beethoven's surveys in the coda often resemble the process of an improvised cadenza). From Haydn, Beethoven took the idea that what sets the coda in motion is unfinished business: it is not so much that the coda tidies up after the main structure is over, but that it realizes the remaining dynamic potential. Beethoven's codas almost never sound like those of his predecessors, but they contain little that cannot be understood as a radical but logical expansion of their practice. Although it would be a mistake to underestimate the originality of Beethoven's expansion—his practice may have been logical but it was unpredictable—it does not help understanding to posit any fundamental break with their styles.

Two symphonic examples may be given. The coda of the Seventh Symphony begins (bar 389) as if it were going to be a parallel to the end of the exposition and the opening of the development at bar 177, and we are only warned that something different is afoot when the upward scale does not continue *fortissimo* but descends *subito piano:*

END OF EXPOSITION

END OF RECAPITULATION AND OPENING OF CODA

The inspiration for the first bars of this coda is found a few pages after the end of the exposition; it is the most electrifying moment in the development, when for two bars we have no idea what the harmony can be. This is perhaps the most ruthless of Beethoven's modulations:

This sudden shift is doubly recalled at the beginning of the coda, but transposed for resolution. The original progression:

now appears as

drawn down to a 6/4 tonic triad. The rest of the movement (there are still forty-seven bars left) largely consists of tonic and dominant harmonies—although no one had ever conceived an alternation of tonic and dominant like Beethoven's in bars 401 and 402, which he repeats a dozen times until he arrives at a more normal cadence.

The coda to the finale of the Eighth Symphony is immense, 235 bars, in fact, almost as long as the rest of the movement. Some commen-

tators are disconcerted by these proportions: Kerman, following Leonard Ratner and others, prefers to call it a second "development" followed
by another recapitulation, although the section in question follows hard
upon a perfectly orthodox recapitulation. It is difficult to see what use is
served by this relabeling: it still leaves the question why Beethoven wanted
a second "development section," if that is what it is. In the end, that is
much the same question as, Why did Beethoven want such an outsize
coda? or What remained unsatisfactory after the regular structure was
complete? Admittedly, to claim that the coda completes unfinished business is close to a tautology, but the formula has the advantage of tying
it to what precedes, of insisting that with Beethoven the coda is not
simply a few good ideas left over for the end. Above all in the case of
the Eighth Symphony finale, the coda may be fruitfully considered as
the goal of the entire movement, as required by the material.

The coda begins with a *pianissimo* statement of the main theme at
the subdominant (this may mean that Beethoven found the allusion to
the subdominant in bars 207–217 of the recapitulation insufficient), but
it breaks it off into fragments, which end angrily. Then a long sequence
of sixty bars, largely employing the circle of fifths, goes from 283 to 342
(the sequential motion really begins at 302 and is only forty bars long,
but the first twenty bars prepare the descending scales that outline the
sequence). This parallels the similar sequence in the development section from bars 111–148. It is in fact basically the same sequence; the
sequence in the development starts and ends on E, the one in the coda
on A. The differences are striking, however. The development uses the
motif of the second half of the main theme:

The coda uses the first half:

Both sections are in fact falling sequences but the development emphasizes a rising motion (falling fifths can be arranged as rising fourths):

*Horn and trumpet parts omitted.

(This motivic structure begins in bar 120: I start it just before the moment when it accelerates, doubling its motion in the last two bars of the example, and it doubles again in the bars that follow.)

The sequence in the coda is made up of rising and falling scales:

and it uses rising fourths only briefly and in passing (in the winds, bars 318–320); the coda's sequence also concentrates on the remote subdominant harmonies like A♭ and D♭, absent from the development.

Both sequences reach a similar climax:

CODA

Here we are on familiar ground. It is Beethoven's standard practice in a recapitulation to resolve a mediant by a submediant, as we know from the "Waldstein" sonata, the Quartet in E♭ major, op. 127, and other works. The parallel of mediant and submediant here indicates that the second passage is therefore not development but recapitulation: its function is to resolve. It is interesting that Beethoven found it necessary to construct a parallel sequence to make the resolution convincing, but even here he is careful to give his sequence the harmonic color of a recapitulation. The principle that the coda resolves the development section had already been fully established by Mozart, and Beethoven's Eighth Symphony is the most massive extension of the idea.

There is, however, still work to be done: the famous C♯ in bar 17 of the main theme must be dealt with:

This C♯ acts almost as an irritant. It reappears without being resolved in the recapitulation; in the coda it is repeated until it causes an explosion (p. 338). Three harmonic interpretations of the C♯ are tried here: D♭ major, G♯ minor, and F♯ minor. The last, and least acceptable, is chosen. The F-major tonic is then reaffirmed by the tympani aided by trumpets and horns, an effect that surpasses the modulation to F♯ in brutality.

385

Tovey called the C♯ in bar 17 a "stumbling-block," the only "puzzling or abnormal feature in the movement" before the coda, and considered the entire coda as "harmonic or enharmonic jokes on this point." Kerman's view of Beethoven's codas as often "the tale of a theme" would be more apt here, although it is not sufficiently general to encompass the way the coda balances mediant with submediant. It is, indeed, possible to view the climax on mediant A major as connected with the C♯ in the initial section. This is not illegitimate, although not fully persuasive, as Beethoven does not normally need that kind of justification to arrive at the mediant. It is, however, clear that the *fortissimo* outburst of D major in bars 345–350 of the coda prepares for the climax in F♯ minor at bar 369. When we consider the violence of this climax, we no longer may judge the length of the coda as unprovoked; we may see it as justified and even demanded by the material. From bar 17 on, the grandest of all Beethoven's codas is a necessity.

Such necessity is always post facto. Whatever is, is right—at least when it comes to the work of a composer in whom we have put our trust. The coda was obviously necessary to Beethoven, because that is the way he wrote it. It seems necessary to us when we have persuaded ourselves that we perceive his reasons, understand his logic. We must accept the fact that so odd a feature as the loud C♯ in bar 17 will act like a magnetic force and produce action at a considerable distance, but we must not hide the other inconvenient fact that it is the analysis that tells us how to hear the music, counsels a certain kind of attention. It is possible, however, to maintain that Beethoven's music itself has from the very earliest time (since 1811, to be exact) stimulated this kind of analysis, provoked a new kind of listening which even transformed the music of his predecessors for future generations. In any case, once we accept—as so many lovers of Beethoven have—that the eccentric C♯ implies a climax three hundred and fifty bars later, and that this climax needs one hundred bars of preparation, it is not hard to swallow the necessity of another hundred bars of resolution afterward. It is clear that Beethoven wanted his splendid F♯ minor triumph and that cramming it into the standard sonata structure, by this time normative, would have destroyed the first half of his movement: an immense coda was the obvious solution—obvious, that is, once it had been composed.

A further eccentricity still remains to be dealt with by the coda in the finale of the Eighth Symphony: the harmonic structure of the second theme. In the final area of stability, the treatment of the second theme has its precedent in the coda of the Mozart Piano Quartet in E♭ major, discussed above (p. 318), as well as in the Mozart Viola Quintet in G minor (see p. 239). In each case, a theme which modulated in both exposition and recapitulation is played wholly at the tonic in the coda. Similarly in the finale of the Eighth Symphony: in the exposition, after six bars of V of V, a new theme appears at the flatted mediant and then at the dominant:

(Ratner[2] points to the fact that the displacement from G to A♭ here parallels the displacement from C to C♯ in bar 17.) These pages reappear
in the recapitulation simply transposed up a fourth, now going from the
flatted submediant (D♭) to the tonic. The coda takes care of this anomaly, absorbing it all into the tonic:

2. Leonard G. Ratner, *Classic Music*, New York, 1980, p. 254.

After this only a small detail remains: the displacement of a half step still causes trouble, reappearing with a subdominant color as is proper towards the end of an eighteenth-century work (and the Eighth Symphony has a determined eighteenth-century character). The half step is now from E♭ to E♮ (G♯ is added in bar 436 to make the relation clearer):

If we are counting recapitulations, this seems to require a third one starting here at bar 438, followed by fifty bars of cadence in stretto style.

It is correct to point out, as Ratner does, that the frequent return of
the main theme in this movement has the character of a rondo, but this
is true of many finales in which the other structural properties of rondo
form have only a small role to play. I have already given the finale of
Beethoven's Appassionata, op. 57, as an example, and should add here
that the coda of this movement has a complete return of the main theme
at the end in the new faster tempo.

To sum up the work of bars 277 to the end of the finale of the Eighth
Symphony, whether we call this section coda or not: The mediant of the
development is. balanced by the submediant; the subdominant area is
given new emphasis (bars 262–278, 314–332, 432–435); the flatted mediant
and flatted submediant of the second theme are resolved wholly into the
tonic, and the implications of the main theme are worked out on a spectacular scale. Finally the tonic area is prolonged and the main theme
recalled at the tonic. This provides us with a summary of most of the
possibilities of the coda from 1770 to 1820, and emphasizes its dependence on the original material and on the development section, as well
as its essential role as a fulfillment of the functions of recapitulation.

To return to our tautology: the coda does the work that is left over.
Does the main theme of the opening Allegro of Beethoven's Quartet in
F major, op. 59 no. 1, contain only passing allusions to the tonic triad in
root position?

The coda fixes that with a decisive tonic drone bass:

Does the first movement of the Hammerklavier Sonata, op. 106, make an unprecedented opposition on a large scale between the tonic B♭ major and the astonishing modulation to B minor in the recapitulation (bars 266–270)? The coda works this out in detail with a C♭-B♭ trill:

and then sixteen bars of written-out trill on G♭ and F, with an insistently dissonant series of clashes:

Beethoven goes beyond these principles in the coda of the Ninth Symphony, where he introduces a new theme at the end of the first movement (bars 513–531), and this example is followed by Brahms in the coda to the first movement of his Second Symphony. The coda to the finale of Brahms' Third Symphony is an occasion for a return to the opening theme of the first movement, but this example of cyclic form is based on the practice of Mendelssohn, principally in the String Quartet in A minor and the Piano Sonata in E major. There was also the example of Schumann's Quintet for Piano and Strings in B♭ major, where the coda of the finale triumphantly exhibits the main theme of the first movement in a fugue. Codas that have little or nothing to do with the preceding sections are found in Hummel, Schumann, and many others, but at this point it seems practical to declare that we have left the various range of sonata forms behind, and that new forces are coming into play.

XIII

Beethoven and Schubert

THE MODEL FOR THE first decade of the nineteenth century was Mozart: it was he, rather than Haydn, who determined the form the sonata was to take except in France, where Haydn's example remained influential in the music of Méhul and Cherubini. From this time on, we may therefore speak of a standard form, largely a generalization and a misinterpretation of Mozart by Beethoven's generation. This is the standard form defined in the opening pages of this book. By 1810 it was generally believed that Haydn had invented the new instrumental style and that Mozart had perfected it.

Such a myth, while necessary to an understanding of the nineteenth century—it became an essential part of history—already falsifies our understanding of the turn of the century, where in the music of composers like Clementi (in his last works) and Dussek there is a renewed interest in concentrating expression in ornament, in the coloristic possibilities of texture, and in the dramatic gestures afforded by striking virtuoso passage work. There is also an extraordinary elaboration of detail in the works of Weber and Hummel, elaboration which creates a relaxed serenity not attainable in the more tightly organized sonata style of the eighteenth century. Large instrumental forms, however, become a classicistic genre; at first the works of Mozart and then, later, of Hummel and of early and middle-period Beethoven are taken as models. There is, above all, an attempt to enlarge these forms, to increase the length of the sections while keeping some of the proportions of the individual phrase. This classicizing tendency is already noticeable in early Beethoven, and in Schubert's chamber works as well as in his sonatas and symphonies. Basic to it then is a conception of sonata form as essentially melodic; the exposition becomes a succession of themes, separated by connecting developments.

Beethoven's escape from the classicizing process is confirmed in the sonatas opus 31 and in the *Eroica*. Before that, his works were frequently based clearly on Mozartean models, such as the Piano Concerto no. 1 and the Quartet in A major, op. 18 no. 5. Some of the early works are constructed loosely by contrast of theme, the relation of tonic and dominant weakened by long chromatic transitions, as in the Piano Sonata in A major, op. 2 no. 2. The *Eroica* reaffirms the direct tonic-dominant binary opposition, which he thereafter retained. He experimented, however, for the rest of his life, with substitutes for the dominant: generally the mediant and submediant (e.g., opus 53, opus 106, opus 127). But these mediants and submediants function within the large system as dominants; that is, they create a long-range dissonance against the tonic and so provide the tension for a move towards a central climax. In addition, their appearance is always prepared so that the modulation creates a dissonance of greater power and excitement than the usual dominant without disturbing the harmonic unity.

I have treated Beethoven throughout as if he were a late eighteenth-century composer. The emotional climate of his music, of course, is that of the Napoleonic and post-Napoleonic eras, and so is its ideological content. Jens Peter Larsen insists that a stylistic cut must be made between Beethoven and his predecessors because Beethoven's music is so much louder than theirs. Even if Mozart liked his music much louder than we sometimes believe (he was delighted when he had forty violins and twelve double basses for a symphony), there is no question that Beethoven made much more noise—although not nearly as much as a contemporary French composer like Méhul or Lesueur when they gave him the proper massed forces for a patriotic holiday piece. Nevertheless, it seems to me that the structure and style of Beethoven's music are best understood as an extension of Haydn and Mozart. In fact, it is the works of Beethoven's final period that are fundamentally most akin to classical Viennese style, in spite of their obvious personal idiosyncracies—perhaps, indeed, because of them.

The tonal language was changing during Beethoven's lifetime; above all, the subdominant lost its antithetical function of opposition to the dominant, and became only another closely related key. If Beethoven's work remains intelligible only as a part and extension of the eighteenth-century tradition of sonata style, it is largely because he observes that classical distinction. Not once does he use the subdominant in an exposition as Schubert did. Above all, Beethoven retains the classical sense of the resolution of large-scale dissonance by the reestablishment of a symmetrical equilibrium.

His careful resolution of the mediant and submediant substitutes for the dominant is characteristic. The exposition of the *Waldstein* goes from C major to E major. The process of resolution in the recapitulation is elaborate; the opening of the second group is played first in the submediant A major (as a symmetrical balance to the mediant E), then in A minor, and finally in C major, making the resolution absolute. The opening of the recapitulation, moreover, contains, at the second phrase, the traditional secondary development with a move to the subdominant side quoted above (p. 290).

This sense of the resolution of dissonant material persists in all of Beethoven's works and sets him apart from his contemporaries. The first movement of the *Eroica* Symphony contains apparently new thematic material that is heard in the remote keys of E minor and A minor. The material cannot, without absurdity, be played in the major, so Beethoven takes special measures to resolve it: at the beginning of the coda it is heard first in F minor, the relative minor of the subdominant, and then in the tonic minor (E♭) as an introduction to an incredibly long passage that does little except to play the main theme with tonic and dominant harmonies over and over again in E♭ major.[1]

Perhaps the most astonishing of Beethoven's sonata resolutions is in the first movement of the Quartet, op. 132. The exposition goes from tonic to submediant (A minor to F major); the subdominant suggestion of the F major which is slight here is offset after a very brief development by a repetition of the exposition from dominant to mediant (E minor to C major). Both first and second groups are then elaborately resolved in the tonic. The middle section acts harmonically as a development and thematically as a recapitulation, which then calls up a *second* recapitulation, this time at the tonic but with thematic developments.[2]

The works of Beethoven's last period, indeed, often represent a contraction or even a distillation of classical procedure rather than an

---

1. In a very generous review of the first edition of this book, Joseph Kerman comments on this passage: "In a symphony called 'heroic' the emotional climate cannot, I believe, be separated off from form and style as clearly as Rosen would like." He adds in a note: "The *Eroica* has, in fact, appalled many listeners . . . Schoenberg frowned on the beginning of the development, which he said aims for 'greater contrasts than structural considerations require'. . . . Schenker could not get himself to consider the coda . . ." It would seem that the centers of outrageous invention here are in the development section and the coda, which are closely related, and that Kerman's conclusion that "something appears to have gone wrong with symmetrical equilibrium here" is unwarranted. The extraordinary coda is called forth as a counterweight to the equally extraordinary development.

2. There are comparable structures in Haydn, notably Symphonies nos. 75 and 89, where the development sections retain the thematic order of the exposition but with the harmonic structure of a development, and the recapitulations remain in the tonic but develop the themes, changing their order.

expansion. The opening of the Sonata in E major, op. 109 (1820) shows this determination to abbreviate without losing anything:

This contains the entire first group (4 bars), beginning of counter-statement (1 bar), bridge passage (3 bars), and opening of the second group. No one has ever done it so swiftly.

For these reasons it may be justly claimed, as Tovey did, that Bee-thoven's innovations are largely a conflation of Haydn's and Mozart's different methods, and that he is best comprehended within their tradi-tion; to Haydn's dynamic sense of continuous motivic development he added Mozart's feeling for long-range movement and the massive treat-ment of subsidiary key areas. Moreover, he attached the long-range movement more directly and more firmly to the motivic detail, deriving the preparation of the large stable areas from the themes through his use of motifs based on simple triads. In this respect above all Beethoven stood almost alone in his time: as the underlying material in the works of all his contemporaries grew more complex and more chromatic, the basic motifs of Beethoven's music became simpler and more diatonic, very often the fundamental elements of the tonal language itself.

This enabled him to continue and expand sonata style, making the polarization more explosive by his use of mediant relationships, and expanding the development section to lengths never before tried (Bee-thoven's expositions remain, in length, on a Mozartian scale). He was also the last great master of heterogeneous textures, so essential to the sonata, in an age when the homogeneous textures of the early eigh-teenth century were beginning to come back into fashion. More than his predecessors, Beethoven was able to make rhythmic iteration (sometimes almost obsessive in his work) do the main work in the creation of both tension and resolution. By his achievement he raised the prestige of the sonata form to an eminence that made it the major challenge to every composer for more than a century to come.

Schubert, on the other hand, represents a break with classical procedure in many aspects of his instrumental works, including those in sonata form. This is particularly striking in the early period. The first movement of the Sonata for Piano and Violin in G minor, op. 137 no. 3 (D. 408) of 1816 has the following structure:

Exposition:	First theme	G minor	18 bars
	Second theme	Bb major (III)	14 bars
	Third theme	Eb major (VI)	19 bars
"Development":	Transition	G minor →Db major (!)	
	(based on first theme)		12 bars
	Fourth theme	Db major	10 bars
	transition		11 bars
Recapitulation:	First theme	G minor	14 bars
	transition	→IV →VI	7 bars
	Second theme	Eb major (VI)	14 bars
	transition	→III	3 bars
	Third theme	Bb major (III)	12 bars
		→G minor	
	First theme	G minor	4 bars

Even if we were to call this a sonata form for lack of a better term, its distance from classical precedure is evident and so is its looseness. There are important analogies with classical technique: the first and third themes are related, the submediant and mediant of the reprise mirror the reverse relationship of the exposition (a kind of distant echo of Beethoven's practice, with none of its rigor). But the form is more a successive contrast of themes and keys colorfully arranged than anything that resembles a sonata before 1800. It is none the worse for being what it is, and, in fact, Schubert here breaks more boldly with tradition than Beethoven. A work like this, however, reveals none of the mastery that Schubert had already shown with the *Lied.*

Schubert was to win that mastery of instrumental forms later, and he acquired exactly as much classical technique as he needed. What he never lost was a classicistic dependence on models. This is natural for a young composer. The finale of his early Quartet in D major (D. 74) of 1813 is a flagrant plagiarism of Mozart's *Paris* Symphony, K. 297:

(Mozart)

(Schubert)

This is no doubt the way every composer learns his craft. But similar examples can be found from the last years of Schubert's life in his numerous reminiscences of Beethoven's opus 28 and opus 31 in the last three piano sonatas. Some of the borrowings are transformed into pure Schubert; the source is then irrelevant.

This characteristic distinguishes the later borrowings of Schubert from those of Beethoven after the *Eroica*. Beethoven adapted his sources (generally from Mozart) to more dramatic purpose: he heightened their effect, made them more powerful, increased their range. With Schubert, when the source is not irrelevant—a kind of involuntary memory, an exterior stimulus to his creative imagination—the adaptation is often a failure. Beethoven's Piano Concerto no. 4 in G major stands up well to Mozart's Concertos K. 453 and 503, from which it borrows. The beautiful slow movement of Schubert's Grand Duo is slightly diminished by the way it recalls Beethoven's Symphonies nos. 2 and 5; the sources are unfortunately relevant for once. Beethoven appropriates what he found elsewhere; Schubert continued to use other works as models.

Unlike Beethoven, Schubert broke at times with the classical opposition between dominant and subdominant—in this, he is the true precursor of the romantic generation born around 1810. The finale of his Quartet in Bb major of 1812 has its second group in IV, and the Quartet in G minor of 1815 has a finale in which the binary scheme is:

I-IV, V-I

a form he used later in the finale of the *Trout* Quintet of 1819. To Schubert, and later to Schumann, there was nothing absurd about an exposition that went from I to IV. The opening of a recapitulation in IV is also used more frequently by Schubert than by any other composer. It is significant that he abandoned both these procedures in his last works, in which the handling of classical form is at its finest.

Schubert's innovations in sonata forms are less extensions of classical style than completely new inventions, which lead to a genuinely new style—at least one that cannot easily be subsumed in classical terms. His handling of tonality in expositions and his use of sequence have been treated above (pp. 256–61, 276). There is room here to mention one more innovation, perhaps the greatest of all: the oscillation between two tonal levels to achieve a kind of stasis. Two examples from the last piano sonatas show this new art; the first is the opening of the development of the A-major Sonata (D. 959) of 1828:

Schubert uses his developments to write new melodies with the motifs of the exposition. The periodic phrase here is, in fact, more regular than that of the exposition, but the harmony of these periods is an apparent motion that hides the fact that only in bars 168–70 is there any real movement—and there we find, too, the first break in a series of rigid five-bar phrases:

131–135	C major ⟶ B major
136–40	B major ⟶ C major
141–45	C major ⟶ B major
146–50	B major ⟶ C major
151–55	C major ⟶ B minor
156–60	B minor ⟶ C major
161–65	C minor
166–67	echo of last two bars
168–72	⟶ A minor
173–79	transposition to A minor of bars 161–67.
180	pedal point on dominant to prepare recapitulation

There is an oscillation of C to B until the tonic minor enters with a break in the phrase rhythm. The absence of real harmonic movement creates a remarkable tension, but it is not the tension of the traditional classical development; we wait for something to happen, but it is not a preparation for a tonic return or of a cadence of any kind. The return of the tonic (bar 168), in fact, is not felt as such; the dominant pedal that follows this passage, however, is the more conventional preparation that appears at last. In fact, it prepares for something which is already there.

The development section of the Sonata in B♭ major is more radical still. There the stasis is the actual preparation for the return of I at the end of the development.

The oscillation is between D minor and Bb major, and the dominant, F, is introduced at first in such a way to remove its character as a dominant: in bars 176 and 182, the F-major triad has all its conventional power removed from it, and V⁷ of V (end of 177 and 183) leads only to D minor. The tonic is introduced only as an alternative plane of sonority to D minor in bar 192, a lower plane, indeed, which diminishes at once to *ppp*. The pendulum swing back to D minor is marked by a crescendo. The return of I is finally accomplished by the *sforzando* V⁷ in bar 202.

The physical effect of such passages is like nothing in music before: composers have often attempted to achieve it since then. It was probably Brahms who came closest to success, in his attempt to arrest all movement with the augmentations at the opening of the reprise of his Symphony no. 4 in E minor, although the exhausted dying away at the end of some of Mendelssohn's developments is a related contemporary phenomenon (see the development section of the early Piano Quartet in B minor of 1823, dedicated to Goethe).

XIV ♫ Sonata Form after Beethoven

WHEN SONATA FORM did not yet exist, it had a history—the history of eighteenth-century musical style. Once it had been called into existence by early nineteenth-century theory, history was no longer possible for it; it was defined, fixed, and unalterable. Except for a few small and unimportant details, sonata form will be for all eternity what Czerny said it was.

There is, of course, the history of what individual composers did with the form, but there is little continuity to this kind of history—it stops with each practitioner, and starts all over again from the beginning with the next. Even its most influential exponents, like Brahms, could not change the form as Haydn or C. P. E. Bach had: after Brahms, sonata form remained what it had been before him. There is, however, the history of its prestige.

A good deal of both instruction and entertainment may be found in the way individual composers from 1830 to the present day came to terms with this powerful form in a whole variety of styles, none of which were especially suitable for dealing with it. This history is irremediably discontinuous because sonata form is largely irrelevant to the history of nineteenth- and twentieth-century styles; it does not generate these styles, and is not altered by them.

The only way to overcome this discontinuity would be to take up each successive change in the language of music and show how it became more or less difficult to manage the form at each point. It would need a book many times the length of this one even to sketch such an approach, which amounts to nothing less than a history of musical style from the death of Beethoven until today. In addition, there is a problem in the choice of examples. For the eighteenth century, one can find examples of the still-developing forms of the sonata that are representative in one of two ways and which complement each other: the examples may represent the stereotyped, normal, stylistic practice at a given moment, or they may represent the extremes to which the style can be taken. No such exemplary choices can be found for the period after Beethoven. The stereotypes of sonata construction in the nineteenth and twentieth centuries are representative not so much of a developing musical language as of the individual composer's laziness or despair. The extreme example, similarly, rarely transcends its localized individual interest to reflect even on the composer's immediate contemporaries. Brahms's magnificent success with sonata form does not illuminate Wagner's absolute indifference to it (except for an early essay). On the other hand, to take two contemporary composers who both employed the form throughout their lives, Brahms and Bruckner, a comparison tells us little about the form but only a good deal about their different relationship to Schubert and Beethoven.

In sum, while much of the history of music from 1740 to 1828 can be written in terms of developing and changing sonata techniques, any similar attempt for what follows is doomed either to create a false context in which all their details are misread, or to present scattered details out of any context, ordered only by chronology and therefore without genuine historical understanding. In what follows I have tried, succinctly, to indicate only a few of the problems. They largely suggest the following generalization: the prestige of the form was a conservative force in the history of Romantic and post-Romantic music, and it acted as a brake on the most revolutionary developments. It also, indeed, sometimes provided a well-built but artificially designed channel for the newer modes of expression. Yet the discontinuity in the history of sonata form has an odd consequence: the most original uses of the form—those of Brahms and Bartók among others—do not take over from the work of the previous generation and build on what they have done but return to Haydn, Mozart, Beethoven, and Schubert.

After Beethoven, the sonata was the vehicle of the sublime. It played the same role in music as the epic in poetry, and the large historical fresco in painting. The proof of craftsmanship was the fugue, but the proof of greatness was the sonata. Only through the sonata, it seemed, could the highest musical ambitions be realized. The opera, because of its extramusical aspects, was only a second best. Pure music in its highest state was sonata.

The coda of the last movement of Hummel's Sonata in F minor, op. 20, betrays these aspirations:

It is clear that Hummel is quoting the finale of the *Jupiter* Symphony: it is less clear whether he is varying it on purpose, or whether he doesn't remember exactly how it goes—at any rate, it is difficult to see the purpose of his minor alterations. Quotation, not imitation, is the form of homage here, and this is very different from Schubert's practice. Hummel quotes the *Jupiter* because it is a famous masterpiece and elevates his coda into the empyrean.

The opening of Brahms's op. 1 in C major makes a similar bow and with similar pretensions:

As Brahms would have said, any ass can see that this is Beethoven's op. 106 in Bb major, the *Hammerklavier*, and for those too dense to take the hint at once, the second phrase starts it again, this time in Bb major. This may be opus 1, but it is Sonata no. 4 on the manuscript; that means (since the second Sonata in F♯ minor was written before this) that there were two piano sonatas that Brahms destroyed before he felt secure enough to publish one in which he could quote the *Hammerklavier* with impunity. For the same reason, he destroyed all his symphonies before no. 1, in which a quotation from Beethoven's Ninth was displayed for all to hear. Behind many nineteenth-century sonata forms—most of Brahms's, for example—there is a specific model, both an ideal and a guide.

For Brahms, sonata form was a congenial outlet for his gifts. For many of the composers born in the generation before him—Chopin, Schumann, Liszt, Berlioz—the form was less natural. But they could not do without its prestige. After having proclaimed that the sonata was dead and that one could not go on repeating the same forms forever, Schumann, only a few years later, lamented that there were too many composers who could write short pieces—nocturnes, songs, and so forth; what was needed was a composer of sonatas, symphonies, and quartets—that is, of sonata forms. The difficulty was that the musical language and the sense of form had changed significantly by 1825.

The Romantic generation turned back to an early eighteenth-century, or Baroque, sense of key relations. For Bach, a tonality was more closely linked with its relative minor than with the tonic minor. D major and B minor were more or less the same key for him, while B minor and B major were very different (even though a piece in B minor may end with a major triad). Not so for the later eighteenth century; having the same tonic note was far more important for Haydn than having the same notes of the diatonic scale.

Sonata style insisted on a sharp focus on the tonic. The Romantics saw the tremendous advantages offered by a fuzzier system. It had become possible to integrate music in a general tonal area, rather than in a clearly defined and specific tonality. The *Kreisleriana*, the *Davidsbündlertänze* and the *Dichterliebe* of Schumann, as well as the Second Ballade of Chopin (in F major/A minor), each create a tonal unity although a central tonality is not focused. The changed relation of minor to relative major reveals this even more strikingly: for Chopin, in the F-minor/A♭-major Fantasie and the B♭-minor/D♭-major Scherzo, they are more or less the same key, as they are for Schumann in "Aveu" from *Carnaval* and in other works.

Since a large number, perhaps the majority, of Romantic sonata forms are in the minor mode, they are obliged by classical rules to go to the relative major. In terms of the more modern Romantic sensibility, they are not going anywhere at all, and no modulation and consequently no polarization takes place.

Various remedies were tried. In his beautiful Sonata for Piano in F♯ minor, Schumann used a variant of the three-key exposition; between F♯ minor and the conventional A major, he placed a third key as far from A major as he could go: E♭ minor. The move from E♭ minor to A major is a series of descending sequences. It is impossible to read into them the kind of close harmonic relationship between the second and third keys that prevailed in the examples from Beethoven and Schubert. For Schumann, it is not an opposition or polarization that defines his exposition; what counts for him is creating a sense of distance. Paradoxically, the move to A major at the end of the exposition of this work has the sense of return.

We must turn to the finale of this Sonata in F♯ minor, to make these relationships clear: both the distant tritone opposition of E♭/A and the ambiguity of F♯ minor/A major reappear, and on an even larger scale. The form of the last movement is one we have met with before (see p. 112): The sonata rondo without development. The essential sonata technique is in the complete rewriting of a very long exposition in order to bring it back to the tonic, but there are some astonishing anomalies which reveal the inadaptability of Schumann's thought to the traditional sonata patterns. (*Text continues on p. 380.*)

Finale
Allegro un poco maestoso M.M ♩ 116

TRANSITION

The first of these anomalies is the sixteen-bar main theme *A*, which is in both F# minor and A major, and, in fact, much more in A major. It has two cadences (bars 8 and 16), both solidly leading to an A-major triad. A new transitional theme *B* (bars 17–24) sets up the tritone opposition by modulating quickly from A minor to Eb major. This fundamentally unclassical opposition is set up almost as a matter of fact, and no justification is attempted—by Schumann's aesthetic none was necessary. A group of themes in E♭ major accordingly follow, some derived from the transitional bars: C^1 (bars 25–32), D (32–38), C^1 (39–42) and C^2 (43–49); the last leads to C minor. At this point the main theme, which went from F♯ minor to A major, is played through, now transposed to C minor/E♭ major. The tritone opposition is confirmed. Note that this tritone opposition is not derived from the thematic material but imposed on it.

The tritone is now reversed: the transitional bars B, which originally went from A minor to E♭ major, now reappear leading from E♭ minor to A major. The themes of the second group reappear, varied and oscillating between F♯ minor and A major. The key of A major appears to be confirmed by bar 114, and there is a long brilliant closing section of the sonata-rondo exposition in A major—that suddenly finishes inconclusively and weakly in F♯ minor (bar 159). One of Schumann's loveliest passages leads to the dominant of F♯ minor, and the preparation of the return of the main theme starts (bar 177) with a variant of the theme itself. The return of the theme is straightforward, closing as before in A major.

This two-hundred-bar pattern is now recapitulated, largely unvaried but with some surprising changes in tonal structure. The transitional theme B goes once more from A minor to E♭ major but suddenly swerves to C major. The second group of themes (C^1, D^1, C^1, and C^2) is now repeated in C major, and the main theme returns in A minor/C major. This adds another tritone relationship, F♯/C♮, also external to the thematic material.

The eight-bar transitional theme does not return, but is replaced by eight bars of the second theme C^1 now played without any preparation in E♭ major. The whole of the passage in the exposition from bars 74 to 159 is now transposed the distance of a tritone from A major to E♭ major (bars 262–350), and it should now be clear that this relation is the fundamental one in the structure. Only towards the end, one bar (342) is added in the middle of a modulating sequence, so that it comes out a whole tone lower, finishing (bar 350) not in C minor (which would parallel the F♯ minor of bar 159) but in B♭ minor. It is odd, indeed, for a large structure to depend on an insignificant detail, on one extra bar in a long sequence.

Bars 351–96 now recapitulate bars 160–89, again with one change: B♭ minor does not lead to its own dominant, but is used itself as a dominant to prepare the return of the theme in E♭ minor (D♯ minor). Since the main theme went first from F♯ minor to A major, it now simply goes from D♯ minor to the F-major tonic. One might say that this moment is, in extraordinary fashion, the first intimation that F♯ is the tonic of this movement (and the sixty bars of coda that follow are the only ones solidly in the key of F♯).

I give a summary of the parallels for convenience:

	Exposition			Recapitulation	
Bars	Theme	Key	Bars	Theme	Key
1–16	A	F♯ minor/A major	190–205	A	F♯ minor/A major
17–24	B	A minor → E♭ major	206–13	B	A minor → E♭ major → C major
25–32	C¹	E♭ major	214–21	C¹	C major
32–38	D	E♭ major	221–27	D	C major
39–42	C¹	E major (ii over V)	228–31	C¹	C major (ii over V)
43–49	C²	E♭ major → C minor	232–38	C²	C major → A minor
50–65	A	C minor/E♭ major	239–54	A	A minor/C major
66–73	B	E♭ minor → A major	255–62	C¹	E♭ major
74–85	D	A major →F♯ minor	262–75	D	E♭ major → C minor
86–97	C³	F♯ minor	276–87	C³	C minor
98–114	C⁴	→ A major	288–304	C⁴	→ E♭ major
114–25	E	A major	304–15	E	E♭ major
126–34	F	A major	316–24	F	E♭ major
134–42	G	A major	324–32	G	E♭ major
142–59	H	18 bars of modulation → F♯minor	332–50	H	19 bars of modulation → B♭minor
160–76	I	F♯ minor	351–67	I	B♭ minor
177–89	Transition	V of F♯ minor	368–80	Transition	V of E♭ minor
			381–96	A	E♭ minor (D♯ minor)/F♯ major
			397–end	coda	F♯ major

The only lapses in the parallel structure of the recapitulation are in bars 213, 255–62, and 342. The last-mentioned bar is buried in the middle of a long set of sequences, and the anomaly is almost imperceptible.

The large-scale tritone structure can be best seen by noting all the successive appearances of the main theme:

Since this structure is not derived thematically, and since (at least before Schoenberg) in no sense can tonalities a tritone apart take on the functions of a tonic and dominant even in rudimentary fashion, this tritone relationship can be heard only in those astonishing short-range modulations (Theme B, bars 17–24, 66–73, and 206–13). One can hardly speak of the polarization so vital to the eighteenth-century sonata forms. The ambiguity of the F♯ minor/A major would already preclude that.

The relation of exposition to recapitulation in this movement has been reconceived by Schumann and laid out as a gigantic sequence supported by internal sequences. Exposition as opposition and recapitulation as resolution have almost disappeared. Indeed, whether the tonal center be held as either F♯ minor or A major, the "recapitulation" almost entirely in C major and E♭ major is structurally more dissonant than the "exposition" in E♭ major and A major. Resolution is pushed off as far as possible in a work of such dimensions.

Looking back at the earlier movements, we can see that they too reveal the ambiguity of a minor key with its relative major that we have found here. The opening section of the scherzo goes to the remote key of the flatted leading tone:

except that it does not appear to be a remote key. The sixteen-bar phrase goes from F♯ minor to E major. By classical tradition it should go to the relative major (A major). Beethoven experimented with mediants, Schubert with the subdominant,[1] but Schumann is both more and less experimental. For him F♯ minor and A major are almost equivalent. If the scherzo opened in A major rather than F♯ minor, it would go traditionally to E major, and that is what it does.

To illustrate the power of Schumann's attack on classical tonality and on the integrity of classical form in this work requires three quotations from the opening movement: the *Introduzione*; the reappearance of the introduction in the development; and the end of the movement and beginning of the slow movement:

1. See the scherzo of the last Piano Sonata, in B♭ major.

a. Introduzione

b. From the Development Section

c. End of First Movement

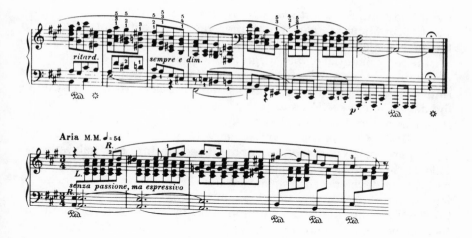

A decade before Mendelssohn's Violin Concerto, Schumann pulls one note out of the final chord of his first movement—not the tonic note of F♯ but of its relative major A—and starts the slow movement with it. This movement opens with the twenty-second bar of the introduction to the first movement and continues for several phrases with its melody. Both these devices compromise, subtly and poetically, the independence of the final tonic cadence and of the form; the first movement does not quite end, the second appears as a continuation of part of a melody played some time before, a memory rather than a new beginning—and a memory that begins in the middle.

The *Introduzione* itself is radically different from any classical introduction to a sonata form. The classical introduction, rhythmically a kind of upbeat to the quick movement, is melodically generally fragmentary, and harmonically always incomplete; it either leads directly into the Allegro after a long dominant pedal, or it ends with a fermata on the dominant. Schumann's *Introduzione* is complete down to a massive tonic cadence with an extraordinary pedal effect. Only the bare fifth left at the end when one raises the pedal hints that the discourse is not finished. By classical standards, it is not an introduction but a song without words, and this makes its startling reappearance in the development section of the Allegro all the more inexplicable by classical aesthetics.

The classical introduction may be tied thematically in its original slow tempo to its Allegro in two ways: it may reappear at an important structural point as a recognizably separate, independent texture—at the coda (as in Mozart's Viola Quintet in D major, K. 593), or at the opening of the development (as in Beethoven's Sonata for Piano in C minor, op. 13, the *Pathétique*). Or it may become part of the thematic material of the Allegro, as in Beethoven's Sonata for Piano in E♭ major, op. 81a (*Les Adieux*). Both methods may be combined, as in Haydn's *Drumroll*

Symphony and Schubert's Symphony no. 7 in C major.[2]

In Schumann's Sonata in F♯ minor, the return of the introduction in the development satisfies none of these conditions. It is not woven into the thematic material of the Allegro, but comes forth as a quotation; it is not, however, an independent texture but is played under the continued figuration of the previous section. It is both an interruption of the development section and part of its process (carrying the harmony from F minor to G♯ minor), like the interruption of the waltz by the *idée fixe* in Berlioz's *Symphonie Fantastique*.

Its arrival divides the development section into two halves; what follows this passage is an unvaried repetition of the first thirty-eight bars of the development transposed up a whole tone. This scheme of large-scale sequence in a development derives, as we have seen (p. 276, from Schubert: the interruption is Schumann's own contribution. Its effectiveness depends on the fact that it is not intelligible in classical terms. It is a formal device whose purpose is to disrupt the form, and it derives its pathos from the way the theme of the introduction forces itself into an alien texture as well as from the character of the theme itself.

This device, like all of the other "anomalies" in Schumann's sonata technique, cannot be properly understood or even discussed in a context of sonata forms alone; it belongs in a more general consideration of Schumann's style, and would demand discussion of similar effects in the *Kreisleriana*, *Carnaval*, *Dichterliebe*, and *Davidsbündlertänze*. However, the same relation to sonata form applies to the work of every other composer since the death of Beethoven. I have dwelt at such length on Schumann's Sonata in F♯ minor because it shows so clearly the difficulties a nineteenth-century composer had with an already-established sonata form. Any other work by Schumann's contemporaries will reveal some of these strains.

For Beethoven the sonata was an *almost* established pattern that he could extraordinarily recreate. That is the paradox of his late style: it appears to be completely free and is, as I have said, closer in most important ways to late eighteenth-century principles than the works of his middle period. After Beethoven, sonata form, like the fugue and ternary or ABA form, was a ready-made pattern, and one of great power and efficiency.

Like the fugue, however, sonata form carried with it certain presuppositions of texture. The most important of these is the thematic (or obbligato) accompaniment (see pp. 181–87). One of the most characteristic inventions of the 1830s, therefore, could not be absorbed into the sonata without great difficulty. This invention may be called the he-

---

2. The return of the introduction at the end of Schubert's symphony is at the original tempo, although notated (with longer note values) in the quick tempo. This tells us that the Allegro is approximately twice as fast as the Andante, although this is sometimes not realized in performance.

terophonic accompaniment: the accompanying figuration is a fluid version of the theme. Chopin's Prelude in G major has one example:

Schumann's Fantasie, op. 17, another:

The preparation for the coda of Chopin's Scherzo in C♯ minor, op. 39, offers still another:

This is neither Baroque counterpoint nor the Classical obbligato accompaniment. Accompaniment here is like a superimposed pre-echo, and there is a double version of the same line.

Chopin, however, hardly uses this romantic creation in the sonatas. There the classical technique significantly remains paramount. In the following bars from the development of the Sonata in B♭ minor, op. 35:

the motif of the main theme appears as accompaniment and then accompaniment is interchanged with the principal voice. This is the basic classical technique. In the Sonata in B minor, op. 58, the second phrase of the opening of the exposition shows the same principle at work:

The accompanying figure in bar 11 is derived from the opening motif, but does not assert itself as principal voice. Sonata form remains a conservative force.

For many composers, as for Schumann, the exposition creates not a polarization but only a sense of distance. The polarization is weakened by a chromatic blurring of the approach to the second tonality. In his Sonata in B minor, op. 58, Chopin tried an analogous approach; his model was Hummel's Sonata in F♯ minor. Here is the counterstatement and bridge passage from Hummel's once-famous work:

To get from F♯ minor to A major, Hummel goes through C major and through enough chromatic passagework to blur one's harmonic sense and add a feeling of drama to what the composer evidently thought was a tame excursion. Chopin, similarly, moves from B minor to D major through B♭ major, touching briefly on E♭ minor. Neither B♭ major nor E♭ minor is even faintly established; the music drifts quickly through them by a technique that Chopin acquired in his study of Bach.

The eighteenth-century conception of recapitulation as resolution sometimes disappears. The second theme of Chopin's Concerto no. 2 in F minor, first movement, is never played in the tonic at all, while the second group of Chopin's Concerto no. 1 in E minor is played in the exposition in the tonic major (!), and recapitulated in the mediant. Chopin's key relations in sonata form, however, were more orthodox after he left Poland.[3] Schumann's C-major Fantasie, which he originally planned to call a sonata, has an exposition which goes to the subdominant and a recapitulation in the flat mediant (E♭ major), a key of greater tension.

The heterogeneous textures of the late eighteenth century, as essential to the sonata style as the harmonic polarization which they reinforce, are often abandoned in favor of a unified rhythmic movement, relentless and almost hypnotic. The problem that this created for sonata

3. The exposition of the Sonata in C minor, op. 4, of 1827 never leaves the tonic. Chopin was only sixteen when he wrote it, but it is not the kind of mistake that Mozart would have made when he was six. They evidently did not have very clear ideas about sonatas out there in Warsaw.

form can be seen in the two versions of the first movement of Schumann's Piano Sonata in F minor (the revised form made the dotted rhythm even more unvaried), and in the obsessive rhythms of certain movements of his symphonies.

The generation born around 1810 preferred to place the climax, the point of extreme tension, very near the end of the work. This makes the final area of stability of the sonata uncongenial to them. What they reject, in most cases, is the sense of climax and resolution at the end of the development and the beginning of the recapitulation. In Mendelssohn's most striking works, as I have said, the end of the development is the point of lowest tension, of an extraordinary poetic stillness. The change of function at this crucial point of the form is so radical that only tradition and convenience prevent us from calling this a new form and giving it a new name.

The sonata is a closed, ordered structure. The composers from 1825 to 1850 preferred open forms, and they sought for the effect of improvisation. The attempt to open up the sonata took two basically related directions:

1) The cyclical sonata in which each movement is based on a transformation of the themes of the others. Very slight suggestions of this may be found in Beethoven from the C-minor Symphony on, but it was in the work of Mendelssohn, Schumann, and Berlioz that the most significant developments took place. This influential idea continued through Franck and Tchaikovsky to the present day.

2) The combination of a one-movement and four-movement structure into one amalgam. The suggestion came once again from Beethoven, who used a modulating scheme for the variation structure of the last movement of the Symphony no. 9 to build an allegro-scherzo-development-slow movement-finale, with the key structure of a finale sonata form (submediant substituted for dominant). The Liszt Sonata in B minor is perhaps the most famous example. It, too, has had a durable influence extending to our century, on Schoenberg's *Kammersymphonie* no. 1 and his First Quartet, and on the Third Quartet of Bartók.

The cyclical form was especially suited to nineteenth-century styles as it placed the chief emphasis on thematic relationships, which predominated more and more over harmonic structure. Thematic relations among different movements of a sonata may be of two kinds: implicit and explicit. The explicit form is infrequent before Beethoven and it is rare in his work. Explicit quotations of the theme from one movement in another are found only in the Fifth and Ninth Symphonies, the Cello Sonata in C major, op. 102 no. 1, the Piano Sonata in A major, op. 101, and the Quartet in C♯ minor, op. 131. With the exception of the last example, in all of these the reappearance of a theme from an earlier movement remains absolutely unintegrated in the later one—it retains the character of a quotation. The implicit form is frequent in Beethoven, where often the themes of several or even of all of the movements are clear versions of the same material.

An astonishing example of the explicit form occurs in Schubert's Piano Sonata in A major, D. 959. The first movement opens:

and the finale closes:

with a free cancrizan version of the opening. Brahms repeats this effect, without the cancrizan, at the end of the Symphony no. 3 in F major.

The romantic innovation here (carried further by Tchaikovsky, Franck, and others) was to integrate the explicit quotation from the first movement as part of the later movements, to combine implicit and explicit techniques, in short. In Schubert and Brahms the quotation is as yet only a framing device, but in Tchaikovsky's Symphony no. 4 in F minor, the motto theme enters as the climax of the finale. Later examples (Tchaikovsky's Symphony no. 5 in E minor, Mahler's Symphony no. 4 in G major) integrate the return of themes from the first movement even more completely without allowing them to lose their character as a quotation from an independent movement.

This is not an account of the faults of early Romantic sonata form, but of the stresses to which it was subject. Codified by 1840, the form was now no longer a free development of stylistic principles, but an attempt to reach greatness by imitation of classical models. The results, at their best, attain a noble, expansive, relaxed, and academic beauty unattainable (and unsought for) in the late eighteenth century.

The academicism was magnified by the generation that followed, and so was its success. The music of Brahms once again attempts the closed forms of the eighteenth century; if his patterns lack the variety of those of Haydn, Mozart, and Beethoven, that is because his style is, in part, a distillation of theirs, a careful selection of those procedures that are best suited to the richer texture of Brahms's music and its greater tendency to a syncopated interweaving of phrase structures.

Brahms, however, widened the harmonic range by a concentration in many works on the dominant minor far beyond the grasp of any previous composer. The source once again, however, is Beethoven, in the *Appassionata,* where the secondary tonality to the tonic F minor is as much Ab minor as major. For a late eighteenth-century composer, the dominant minor could only be an interesting chromatic alteration of the dominant major, but in Brahms it becomes a full secondary tonality in its own right within the exposition. The grandest examples are in the opening movements of the Violin Concerto and the Second Piano Concerto. More than any other composer, Brahms exploited the possibilities of overlapping sections, the ambiguities of the boundaries of sonata form. He derived some of his art from his study of Haydn and Mendelssohn, but his expansion of the technique was considerable. The move into the recapitulation of the Viola Quintet in G major, op. 111, of 1891 allows him a beautiful opportunity for blurring the edges:

He begins to establish G major with great ambiguity in bars 100–02 partly as if it were a dominant of C minor but without pressing the point; the shift to E♭ is sudden at the end of 102. It is in the middle of the E♭ chord at the end of bar 105, after two beats of disorienting syncopations, that the cellist begins the main theme. (If he had difficulty making himself heard at the opening of the movement, his troubles are compounded now.) The tonic appears at the opening of bar 106 but there is no real cadence on I until bar 107. Entrance of theme, arrival of I, and cadence are all out of phase—and these staggered effects are underlined by the syncopations and sudden shift of theme from cello to first violin (bar 107).

This blurring is even applied to the very opening of a work. Opus 111 was intended to be Brahms's farewell to music, but his interest in composition revived in some works for the clarinet. The opening of the Clarinet Quintet, op. 115, of 1892 is a homage to Haydn's Quartet in B minor, op. 33 no. 1, (see pp. 179–80): as in the model, the opening bars could be D major:

There is no tonic chord in root position until bar 18: it is neatly evaded in bar 3, and the possibility of D major returns in bars 4–7. The theme that appears at bar 14 is first presented on a dominant pedal. The technique is fluid, the affirmation of B minor done so delicately that the full tonic chords of bar 25 seem like a new beginning. The glory of Brahms's academicism is his almost complete transformation of his models.

Contemporary with Brahms's work, we find an increasing taste for chromaticism that makes the tonal orientation of a sonata exposition increasingly hard to realize. The first and second themes of Bruckner's Symphony no. 7 in E major show the way chromaticism was handled for two parts of an exposition:

a. FIRST THEME

The first theme so firmly outlines the tonic triad that E major is fixed throughout the modulations that follow in spite of the intense leaning towards B major. The second theme is able to take this B major for granted, but harmonic change is here so continuous, the modulations so fast that the opposition is not of tonality but of harmonic character and texture. By the end of the century the chromaticism is pervasive and all sense of harmonic opposition completely disappears with Reger and Scriabin.

After Brahms, sonata form provided a loosely constructed model, a pattern that gave free access to the imitation of the classics. The scheme of exposition, development, and return was a useful one, and it could be variously interpreted. In general, it was considered a variant of ternary form, an ABA scheme in which the first A section does not really conclude, and the B section is characterized by fragmentation, thematic development, and a dramatic texture. Sometimes only part of the scheme may be present. Stravinsky's Sonata for Piano has a central development but is otherwise clearly in concerto grosso form. The tonal orientation can often be very loose even when, for the sake of symmetry, the movement begins and ends in the same key: Hindemith's Sonata no. 3 for Piano in Bb major has a second theme in E minor which is recapitulated in A minor and D minor. Recapitulation is conceived here not as resolution but as a free return of the opening material. By the twentieth century, often the only thing that distinguishes sonata form from a strict ternary or da capo form is its freedom. However, a free symmetrical return of the opening material remains basic to much twentieth-century music.

With non-tonal sonata forms, of course, tonal polarization and resolution disappeared completely; what remains is the thematic structure along with contrasting textures—one contrast between the relative simplicity of the outer section and the more intense center, and another within the exposition to distinguish first and second themes. A substitution for tonal orientation is sometimes devised in serial works: Schoenberg's String Quartet no. 3, for example, uses a transposition of the row a fifth down for the second theme of the exposition, the relation of the fifth being derived directly from the row invented for this work.

The first atonal sonata form is the third of Alban Berg's Three Pieces for Orchestra of 1913. In his *Lulu*, sonata form is used to characterize the important role of Dr. Schoen. Since the pattern is worked out intermittently through various scenes of the first two acts, it is difficult to hear it as an integral form. The purely textural aspect is now supreme: sonata form for Berg here is a texture characterized by thematic development, using the classical procedures of such development; and exposition and return have necessarily a limited effect placed so far from each other.

Elaborate analogues for the tonal structure of sonata form may be created in atonal works. The most masterly are those by Bartók. Quartet no. 5, for example, is atonal at least in its complete evasion of triadic tonality except in the scherzo and in one parodistic phrase in the last movement. A central note takes the place of the central triad (modal would perhaps be a better word than tonal for this system). The displacement of the central note gives the possibility of modulation; and the substitution of an inverted downward motion for an initial rising modulation is a fine parallel of classical resolution.

Exposition
Bars   1–14   Theme I (B♭ as center)
  15–24   Transition (bridge), developmental texture
  25–44   Theme II (C♯ as initial center in bass) and
      return of Theme I with C as its center
  45–58   Theme III (A♮ as center)
      Rising chromatic bass

45   Bb
49   B♮
53   C
54   C♯
55   D
56   Eb

59   Return of Theme I (E♮ as center)

Development
    Bars 63–132   (Return of Theme I (F as center, 126–32)

Recapitulation in reverse order
    Bars 133–46   Theme III inverted (F♯ as center)
                  Descending upper line

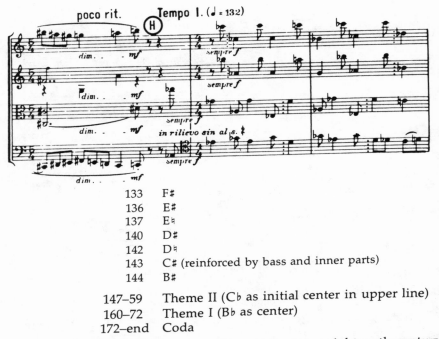

133	F♯
136	E♯
137	E♮
140	D♯
142	D♮
143	C♯ (reinforced by bass and inner parts)
144	B♯

147–59	Theme II (C♭ as initial center in upper line)
160–72	Theme I (B♭ as center)
172–end	Coda

A reverse recapitulation has, as we have seen, many eighteenth-century precedents, and the use of inversion has played a large role in twentieth-century style. In Bartók's Quartet no. 5, inversion clearly functions as a downward chromatic movement which resolves into the initial B♭. The very success of Bartók's structure makes it, like most masterpieces, unsuitable as a model. It is not so much a new version of sonata form as a brilliant twentieth-century metaphor for sonata form.

A doctrinaire classicism remains inherent in the use of sonata form. The Sonata no. 2 of Pierre Boulez, for example, has, like Brahms's opus 1, a dependence on Beethoven's opus 106 acknowledged by explicit quotation. In addition, its opening movement has clearly defined first and second themes, a development, and characteristic elements of recapitulation (including the inversion of part of the exposition) interspersed, as in Haydn's recapitulations, with further development. Elliott Carter has substituted juxtapositions of texture for thematic contrast in a number of works. The symmetry of the form and its latent possibilities of drama made it inevitably attractive to a composer like Prokofiev, who required an easily identifiable thematic structure. For some composers, the form provides a decent cover of respectability for what might otherwise appear to be a frivolous pandering to the virtuoso performer's taste. Even Debussy, who was at first, like Schumann, an implacable enemy of the form, was won over at the end of his life into the kind of classicistic view that sonata form implies today.

Index

Pages with music examples in **bold face**. Bibliographical references indicated by an asterisk.